T0196899

Jesus Is the Light in This Dark World

by: Daniel Evans

WESTBOW
PRESS®
A DIVISION OF THOMAS NELSON
& ZONDERVAN

Scripture taken from the New King James Version®. Copyright © 1982 by Thomas Nelson. Used by permission. All rights reserved.

This book is a work of non-fiction. Unless otherwise noted, the author and the publisher make no explicit guarantees as to the accuracy of the information contained in this book and in some cases, names of people and places have been altered to protect their privacy.

WestBow Press books may be ordered through booksellers or by contacting:

WestBow Press
A Division of Thomas Nelson & Zondervan
1663 Liberty Drive
Bloomington, IN 47403
www.westbowpress.com
1 (866) 928-1240

Because of the dynamic nature of the Internet, any web addresses or links contained in this book may have changed since publication and may no longer be valid. The views expressed in this work are solely those of the author and do not necessarily reflect the views of the publisher, and the publisher hereby disclaims any responsibility for them.

Any people depicted in stock imagery provided by Thinkstock are models, and such images are being used for illustrative purposes only. Certain stock imagery © Thinkstock.

ISBN: 978-1-5127-6745-2 (sc)
ISBN: 978-1-5127-6746-9 (hc)
ISBN: 978-1-5127-6744-5 (e)

Library of Congress Control Number: 2016920510

Print information available on the last page.

WestBow Press rev. date: 1/3/2017

To
those who want the Light of Jesus to shine through
them so that others will accept Him

Contents

Preface

Come *and* hear, all you who fear God,

And I will declare what He has done for my soul.

Psalm 66:16

Preface

I'm just an ordinary layperson, who took the Bible seriously and became deeply in love with Jesus and The Holy Spirit. I am not perfect by any means. Just ask my wife. I'm as unclean as everyone else in this world. My uncleanliness reminds me of Isaiah 64:6.

> But we are all like an unclean *thing,*
> And all our righteousnesses *are* like filthy rags;
> We all fade as a leaf,
> And our iniquities, like the wind,
> Have taken us away.

If I were to reveal all of the sin over the course of my life, then this book would be more than twice as long and would detract from Jesus, who is so awe-inspiring. I am a sinner saved by grace. Although I now live righteously, I am not righteous. Only Jesus is righteous and perfect.

This book is not about me; that's why I decided to show my name in small font size on the book's cover. This book tells God's story through me; what happened spiritually to me. It's all about Jesus and The Holy Spirit coming to me, the wonderful experiences and encounters, how He impacted my life, and what I learned.

He has blessed me so much with His presence, His words, the incredible joy in my heart after actually doing what He wants me to do, and His forgiveness for my daily impurity which is usually pride. God also has a way of humbling me. I can never describe everything that I have experienced with Him, but this book is my attempt at trying to capture the major events.

People have asked me why I have experienced so many encounters with God, and I really don't know, because I have also wondered the same thing. One minister told me that I must have an unbelievable prayer life, but I really don't think so, since I don't know how others pray, or their quality time with Jesus. I pray on a daily basis on my knees, and I try to pray with all my heart. I have noticed that the spiritual experiences occurred after I was baptized in The Holy Spirit. Perhaps, it's because I surrendered to Jesus, asked Him to make decisions for me, and then follow His words. Perhaps, the reason might be revealed in John 14:21.

> He who has My commandments and keeps them, it is he who loves Me. And he who loves Me will be loved by My Father, and I will love him and manifest Myself to him.

I really tried hard to follow all of Jesus' commandments, but I fell short. So, I asked the help of The Holy Spirit. Only by the help of The Holy Spirit, the blood of Jesus and His grace can I follow his commandments. Since Jesus hasn't told me why He has manifested Himself to Me, I really don't know.

If you like to hear in person these wonderful moments with God at your church, mission committee, or other group, just contact my website as shown in the back of the book. *I just love to tell others about Jesus.*

After I was baptized in The Holy Spirit in May 2005, I was dramatically changed; my outlook on life, my worldview, my demeanor, in short *everything* changed. My friends and children noticed that I had become a new person.

I wasn't sure if I should tell others what happened to me, fearing that they would think that I was crazy. This led to this intense pressure inside my head, which made my head feel like it was going to literally burst wide open. Therefore, I had to tell others my testimony, and when I did, God would bless me by filling my heart with incredible joy. He filled me with so much joy, that I couldn't wait to tell someone else. At times, my wife would urge me not to say anything to a new couple, so that my testimony wouldn't deter anyone from becoming new friends with us. Of course, my testimony didn't deter anyone; it actually strengthens our ties with new friends.

After we moved from northern Virginia to Des Moines, I asked Jesus what I should do next, how I could serve Him. His response was for me to write my spiritual experiences and encounters in a book. I haven't written a book before, so I asked The Holy Spirit to help me write this book for Jesus.

I would have never thought of writing a book, since I'm not a writer. **It was Jesus' idea.** He wanted me to write my spiritual experiences in a book. So this is it. I do not boast in any of this – it's just that I am so thankful that Jesus has used me for the will of our Father. *It is my sincere hope that this book will inspire you, so that you will come closer to Jesus and tell others about Jesus, and all of this to glorify Jesus.*

The title comes from my first awe-inspiring vision with Jesus, which is explained in the chapter "Jesus Takes Me Flying", and further explained in my fourth experience "Jesus and The Never-Ending Stream/River of Love". During Jesus' fourth encounter with me, He revealed the purpose of flying with Him was to show me that He is the Light in this dark world and the Way out of it. Therefore, I entitled this book <u>Jesus is the Light in This Dark World</u>. The book's cover depicts Jesus taking me flying. You'll learn more about this event in my life, as well as others, later in this book.

Any and all net profits generated by this book will be donated to Christian homeless shelters. I don't want to make any money off the sales of this book. I would encourage you to donate money to the Nehemiah House in Woodbridge, VA, The Refuge – A Fresh Start in Marshall, MN, or to a Christian homeless shelter in your area. See the last attachment in this book for contact information for the planned Nehemiah House or The Refuge – A Fresh Start. These are the two homeless shelters that Jesus used me to help start.

I have inserted pages for you to capture your thoughts, notes, and comments at the end of each section, which consists of multiple chapters. Use this book as a workbook by underlining sentences, highlighting major points, etc. Use it to assist you in your spiritual journey.

God wired me as an analytical person, so when I was baptized in The Holy Spirit, I started to analyze everything around me. I became more aware of God's involvement in everyday life. I started praying more earnestly with my whole heart. I also started reading The Holy Bible in a focused manner. I fell in love with God's Word, and I was changed from the inside out. Therefore, as visions, words, etc. were received from God, they reminded me of scriptures in the Bible. That's why I have shown a number of Bible verses in this book.

Usually, as I tell others my testimony, they feel inspired and perhaps, you too will feel inspired after reading this book, and then you can tell others your testimony. Jesus may use your testimony to make a difference in some else's life, as well as blessing you.

This reminds me of Jonah, who told his testimony to Nineveh (city of approximately 120,000 at that time), and that they would be overtaken in forty days. When Jonah shared his testimony, it resulted in the people of Nineveh turning from their evil ways and God sparing their lives, as is written in Jonah 3:10:

Then God saw their works that they turned from their evil way; and God relented from the disaster that He had said He would bring upon them, and He did not do it.

This book reveals the times that Jesus and The Holy Spirit came to me, and how those visions/encounters changed my life. Our testimonies are to glorify Jesus, not ourselves. By telling your testimony to others and that Jesus is Lord, this will encourage them to seek Jesus. So tell your testimony today.

Now, let me tell you a little bit about what my life was like before and after baptism in The Holy Spirit.

Part One:
Life Before and After
Baptism in The Holy Spirit

For by one Spirit we were all baptized into one body—
whether Jews or Greeks, whether slaves or free—
and have all been made to drink into one Spirit.

1 Corinthians 12:13

how much more will your heavenly Father give
the Holy Spirit to those who ask Him!

Luke 11:13 (b)

Life Before Baptism in the Holy Spirit

My name is Daniel Evans, and this is God's story of coming to me and working through me.

I was born in an extremely poor area of Omaha, called East Omaha. At the time, there were no paved streets, no indoor plumbing, etc. - just electricity. Even now, it seems that East Omaha is the forgotten part of the city. Sometimes maps of Omaha don't show East Omaha. Some years, East Omaha has been part of Iowa, and other times, it has been in Nebraska, depending on whether the Missouri River changed channels.

When I read that some of the people in The Holy Bible, such as David and Jesus, came from poor areas, I pump my right fist and yell "Yes"!! It just makes me feel good to know that David and others came from humble upbringings.

My mother named me after Daniel in The Holy Bible. She showed me the picture in The Holy Bible of Daniel with two lions, but I really didn't understand it at the time. Later in life, I recognized that your name is important. As I read the book of Daniel, I became excited and could visualize what happened to Daniel in the Old Testament.

When I was about five years old, the Missouri River flooded, and my family moved temporarily to our cousins' house. The city forced us to move by taking our land and house, because they wanted the land to build Abbott Drive to the airport. I remember my father yelling about how we didn't have the money to live somewhere else. We moved to 43rd and Maple Street in

Omaha. During that year, I was baptized at a Methodist church in Loup City, Nebraska. Today, I don't remember my original baptism, since it happened so long ago, but Nancy and I have now been baptized (full immersion) in the River Jordan.

My family consisted of my earthly father, mother, brother, and sister. My mother ironed other people's clothes and decorated cakes to make ends meet, while my dad worked as a welder. I started to deliver weekly newspapers when I was seven years old carrying them in my wagon. I would roll them up, put a rubber band around them, and then walk up to each door and put the paper on the door knob with the rubber band. Then, I worked at a restaurant as a teenager, selling Christmas cards door to door, etc. Work is just a good and natural part of my life. I always felt a need to work.

As a young boy, I attended Clifton Hill Presbyterian Church. When I was about twelve years old, I graduated from confirmation class. Shortly after graduating, I stood in the middle of our living room when no one else was home. I prayed out loud that I would devote my life to Jesus. Then a cone of sunlight (like a spotlight, but it was sunlight) shone through the ceiling onto me. I remember that it felt warm and good. I was amazed that sunlight could come through our roof and ceiling!

Shortly after confirmation class, my dad's anger increased, and then anger became part of my life for many years.

Four years later, when I was sixteen years old, I attended summer school class at Technical High School in Omaha. I didn't need to go to summer school, since I was a good student, but I just wanted to learn more. My mother encouraged me to learn as much as I could. So I attended summer school in the summer between my sophomore and junior years.

As I sat in class on that June morning, I was surprised to see my uncle Bill walk into the class room and whisper something in my teacher's ear. He then told me, as well as the entire class, that my dad had died in an "accident" at his work. Tears flooded my eyes and slowly ran down my face. I seemed to be in a fog or a different dimension. I left school with my uncle Bill, and he drove me home. When I arrived home, I went outside and sat in the front yard, and started to hand trim the grass. I just wanted to be left alone. As others came to console my mother, I continued on my knees cutting the grass with hand shears.

That day changed my life, and my friends said that my personality and temperament became serious after that. My dad was a welder at a local steel company. Someone explained to me that my dad was welding on the corner of a large metal platform that was held up by a crane. I knew that welding causes a lot of sparks, and I was told that my dad was the only one working on the platform. Then, a fellow worker walked in and unhinged the crane. The platform came crashing down to the floor and crushed my dad. As I closely examined what happened, it was clear to me that this guy obviously saw my dad working on the platform, since welding causes a lot of sparks, unhooked the crane, and the side supports gave way crushing my dad. I concluded that it wasn't an accident. My dad's fellow worker staged the "accident", and immediately left work and the state. No further police follow-up work was done, perhaps because my dad was poor and really a nobody.

To this day, I remember the funeral. It was a dark and dreary day, and numerous cars followed the procession to the cemetery. A tent was set up, where many crowded around as the minister conducted the funeral service.

Although my dad occasionally attended church, I don't know if he made it to Heaven or not. I'll find out when I go to Heaven.

After my father's death, I made a huge foundational mistake. My advice is this: don't do what I did next.

I started to question, why God would allow such a terrible event like this to occur? He didn't answer. I started to mentally drift away from God. At that time, my thoughts evolved into an agnostic position, not knowing whether there is a God. Of course, it didn't help that my college roommate John, an atheist at the time, would ask me if I really knew that there was a God.

Looking back, I was judging God, and God won't answer those prayers. If I would have asked God "Who are You? ", God would answer those prayers forever.

My dad's death and my questioning God became a root of bitterness in my heart. See Hebrews 12:14-16:

> Pursue peace with all people, and holiness, without which no one will see the Lord: looking carefully lest anyone fall short of the grace of God; lest any root of bitterness springing up cause trouble, and by this many become defiled; lest there be any fornicator or profane person like Esau, who for one morsel of food sold his birthright.

Anger, bitterness, and lust drifted into my life and remained part of my life until many years later when I was baptized in The Holy Spirit. After my dad was killed, I married, graduated from college, had a wonderful daughter and son, and tried to climb the corporate ladder without really knowing Jesus. I also attended church without involving my heart. And occasionally drinking beer became the new normal for me. This type of life style consumed me for the next thirty years.

Let me tell you about my brother Jack. Jack was five years older than me. I was sixteen years old when my dad was killed, and my brother Jack was twenty-one.

While Jack was in the Navy, he started drinking. After several months at sea, his air-craft carrier would dock on dry land. He would go into the town and hit the bars.

After leaving the Navy, Jack worked for a local utility company as a low-paying ditch digger while experiencing the devastating effects of alcohol. He was married, and they had three boys.

I need to caution you that the following description of my brother's death is graphic and may cause you to feel queasy. If you might feel this way, you can skip over this section.

In his thirties, when Jack was mowing the lawn, he collapsed face first in the front yard. The deafening sirens of the ambulance scorched the neighborhood as it raced his body to the hospital. He had suffered a massive stroke that paralyzed the left side of his body. His lifeless, left arm hung in a sling, as a limp attachment to his shoulder. At times, his arm would smell like a locker room after a hockey game (it's hard to wash yourself with one arm), and he swung his left leg to walk with a cane.

Jack didn't work after suffering the stroke, even though he applied to many companies. He was depressed, had anger issues like our dad, and continued to curl up inside a bottle. His wife divorced him and took the boys with her.

Jack found a small, cheap apartment that at times had cockroaches crawling around in daylight, as well as in the night. After twenty plus years of this solitary existence, he cruelly suffered an aneurism, which killed him. He was cooking in his kitchen, standing next to the counter when his attack occurred. He collapsed, falling down, and hit the edge of the hard kitchen counter with his head, which caused a hemorrhage. Then his lifeless body crumpled to the floor. Jack bled to death through his mouth; spilling blood out onto the kitchen floor.

Several days later, the apartment manager, after receiving complaints of a stench, opened the door of my brother's apartment to find his decaying body on the floor in a pool of blood. The police officer at the scene made a drawing, as part of his notes supporting his report, which he reluctantly showed me, that depicted Jack on the floor with his mouth wide-open. The police officer told me it was the worst, bloodiest scene he had ever witnessed in more than thirty years of working on the police force.

My mom called me, and when I arrived, she asked me to clean up Jack's apartment. I picked up the cleaner, towels, scraper, etc. from mom's house and opened up his apartment to walk into the kitchen, where I found the dried, red, jelly-like blood that appeared to be more than an inch thick in some places. I could clearly see the outline of his head and hair in the dried, jelly-like blood, as well as the volume of blood that flowed out of his mouth. After cleaning up the kitchen floor, I hauled Jack's furniture, as well as a number of rum and Coca-Cola bottles, out to the dumpster in the parking lot.

But on the third day after his death, my mother, while halfway lying on her couch, witnessed in a vision of Jack waving both of his arms wildly, jumping up and down in joy! Jack had made it to Heaven! Standing on Jack's right side was his youngest son, who had previously died in an automobile accident, and Jack was talking to him. Unbelievable. I was surprised that Jack made it to Heaven, because I remember the heavy drinking, at times foul language, and tactless behavior.

But during roughly the last five years of his life, a man drove up to his apartment, picked him up, and took him to church. Then, he didn't seem to be drinking as much, or at least when he called me, he didn't seem to be slurring his words as often.

My mother had a strong vibrant faith in Jesus and a strong will. After she experienced a terrible car accident in southern Missouri with her husband, she told me about her near-death experience.

Mom told me that after the accident, she floated up, out of her body, and traveled at a high rate through a tunnel, while she saw the blur of many faces of people in the tunnel. There was a bright, shining light at the end of the tunnel. Then, she saw the golden streets of Heaven, the exquisite, brightly-colored flowers, and she heard beautiful music. Tears rolled down her face while she shook her head. She retrieved her handkerchief out of her pocket to wipe away the tears in her eyes and running down her cheeks. I asked mom, "Why are you crying?" She replied that she didn't want to come back to earth, and that she wanted to stay in Heaven.

When she came back to earth, she found herself in a crumpled-up car. She tried to get out of the car, but the doors were impossible to open. Suddenly, a man with massive muscles appeared, proceeded to rip the car door clean off of its hinges. Then the paramedics pulled her from the car. She wanted to thank the muscular man, but he had vanished into thin air!

My sister, as a teen-ager, grew up without a dad, but she developed into a wonderful, God fearing woman, who is married with three boys. Even though they are not wealthy, God has blessed them in many ways.

These are most of the major events in my life before I was baptized in the Holy Spirit.

Take a couple of minutes and think back over the major events impacting your life. Have you searched for Jesus? Have you seen God intervening in your life?

If you have time, make your own life chart. Draw the x-axis horizontally and the y-axis vertically. Display age on the bottom x-axis starting from zero to 90. Show positive or negative experiences on the y-axis starting from negative ten to positive ten.

You can show the major events in your life, perhaps starting with your birth with the coordinates (0, 9), where zero on the x-axis represents your birth, and 9 on the y-axis represents a very positive experience. Go ahead and show other major events in your life, such as marriage (another high-point), children, divorce (normally a low-point), etc.

What does your graph look like? How would you describe your life so far? Has God been a part of your life? What would you do different to draw closer to Jesus?

I'm also reminded of Nathanael in John 1:45-51:

> Philip found Nathanael and said to him, "We have found Him of whom Moses in the law, and also the prophets, wrote—Jesus of Nazareth, the son of Joseph."
>
> And Nathanael said to him, "Can anything good come out of Nazareth?"
>
> Philip said to him, "Come and see."
>
> Jesus saw Nathanael coming toward Him, and said of him, "Behold, an Israelite indeed, in whom is no deceit!"
>
> Nathanael said to Him, "How do You know me?"
>
> Jesus answered and said to him, "Before Philip called you, when you were under the fig tree, I saw you."
>
> Nathanael answered and said to Him, "Rabbi, You are the Son of God! You are the King of Israel!"
>
> Jesus answered and said to him, "Because I said to you, 'I saw you under the fig tree,' do you believe? You will see greater things than these." And He said to him, "Most assuredly, I say to you, hereafter you shall see heaven open, and the angels of God ascending and descending upon the Son of Man."

Please note that Nathanael just sat under a fig tree. He wasn't saying anything. I would like to think that Nathanael was reflecting on his life, and he was searching for God. Then, he realized Jesus is the Son of God, and he believed in Him.

Now, let's learn about the next event in my life, which turned out to be the turning point in my life.

Baptism in The Holy Spirit

My wife Nancy encouraged me to go to church with her every week. Before and after church, I would talk with Bill and Marilyn who became our friends.

Bill and Marilyn tried numerous times to convince us to go on the Walk to Emmaus. I said sure, but I never actually signed up. After two years of putting Bill off, he got in my face, and insisted that I go on the Walk to Emmaus. Rather than ruin our friendship, I told him that we would go. Later, he told me that The Holy Spirit was driving him to ask me to attend the Walk to Emmaus.

I didn't know what to expect of the Walk to Emmaus, and I was hesitant about going, since there would be others there that knew The Holy Bible better than I did. I didn't want to look stupid.

Since Bill had recently moved to the Detroit, Michigan area, an Emmaus friend of Bill picked me up on a Thursday evening in May 2005. I was 57 years old. I brought casual clothes, a Holy Bible, shaving equipment, deodorant, tooth paste, and tooth brush.

As he drove me, I mentioned that I hoped that there wasn't much singing, since I don't have a good voice, and I didn't enjoy singing. He chuckled and said that I shouldn't worry about it, but that there would be singing during the Walk to Emmaus.

I also mentioned that I was tired of my job, since I was streamlining the corporation and many would lose their jobs. I didn't receive any additional money for streamlining the corporation, only pats on the back. I was trying to climb the corporate ladder, make more money, and so I dressed professionally. I pretended to be better than others.

Now, I no longer wanted this type of work, and just wanted a job where others would not be losing their jobs - perhaps computer programming.

When I arrived on Thursday evening, I met my roommate Jay. Jay was a quiet man, who was going to be a missionary in Africa for a group called AIM (Africa Inland Mission). AIM AIR is a Christian missionary aviation organization—part of the larger ministry of Africa Inland Mission. He's a pilot, who is now flying supplies and people around Africa. His family is also with him in Africa. I thought to myself "That is really different". I had never met a missionary before, but he was a pleasant, quiet guy.

I won't reveal much about the Walk to Emmaus, since there are a number of wonderful surprises, and I don't want to spoil it for you by telling you everything that happens.

I would strongly encourage you to find a sponsor, sign up and attend the Walk to Emmaus in your city. You can find the closest Walk to Emmaus on the internet, and when it will be held. Check it out, meet your sponsor, sign up, and attend.

It could change your life in a wonderful way. I know, because that's what happened to me. It's actually Jesus and The Holy Spirit that would change your life, and He is at the Walk to Emmaus, if you will open your heart and invite Him in.

At the Walk to Emmaus, everyone was divided up into small groups and sat at their respective table. At our table, which was named Matthew, was our table leader Tim, who is a large, tall man with a long pony tail at the time, an assistant table leader, and two other guys like me who were referred to as pilgrims; for a total of five guys at our table including myself. There are fifteen talks delivered by clergy and lay people over the course of three days, and each table discusses the talks.

After the events of the first evening, we quietly went to our rooms and went to bed. Jay was in prayer and read his Holy Bible before going to sleep. I went to sleep.

On Friday morning, we ate breakfast and went into the large room with tables for each small group. The first talk grabbed my attention, and I was very focused on every word that he said. It seemed like he was talking directly to me. His talk hit me right between my eyes. He said that he placed everything else in this world higher than his faith. He listed a number of examples, such as work, drinking, parties, etc. That was a perfect description of me.

Looking back, the Holy Spirit was starting to work on me. After his talk, our table went into a small room and discussed it.

After a couple more talks that afternoon, Tim asked if any of us wanted to ask Jesus to forgive our sins. I reached out across the table and grasped the hands of another guy who I barely knew. ***I cried out loud and asked Jesus to forgive me for my sins.*** *Tears rolled down my face, as I cried out to Jesus. Then, I experienced an inner feeling that Jesus did forgive my sins!! Unbelievable!*

I had strayed away from God, but He never strayed away from me! By asking Jesus for forgiveness, I was closer to Jesus, even though I didn't fully realize it at the time.

After the talks, table assignments, events, etc. on Saturday, Tim wanted to go into the small chapel and pray. He asked us if we wanted to go with him. We said yes.

Each of us took turns getting on our knees and praying out loud, as the others would stand behind them with their hands on his back; laying of hands. Tim went first, he's a big man, but the emotions and tears flowed freely as he prayed out loud.

Then, it was my turn. As I kneeled down to pray out loud, the other four guys laid their hands on my back. See the picture below, which is a reenactment of laying of hands at the Walk to Emmaus Weekend. Then, after I prayed, Tim prayed, followed by the other guys praying for me out loud.

When Tim was praying out loud for me, *Tim asked for The Holy Spirit to come into my body. That's exactly what happened!* **It was something that I could physically feel.**

This was my first experience with the Holy Spirit. Since then, I have learned that when I 'm in the Holy Spirit, I see things that normally I can't see and hear things that normally I can't hear; plus, there's a tingling sensation throughout my body and it feels like I'm in a different dimension.

At that moment, **I could see inside my body, and I witnessed my heart jump in joy!** *My heart was giddy and did a summersault!! My heart was overflowing with pure joy!*

My heart has never jumped before or since then. I had never experienced anything like that before.

As Tim continued to pray out loud for me, I heard a buzzing noise. I turned my head to the right to find the source of the buzzing sound. Then, I turned my head to the left still trying to locate the buzzing sound.

The palm of Tim's right hand was on my left shoulder. Amazingly, *I witnessed bolts of lightning between Tim's palm and my shoulder!! Wow!! It felt somewhat like electricity flowing throughout my body.*

This feeling is somewhat similar to physical therapists placing electrodes on my skin to relax tense muscles. The *surging of electricity throughout my entire body, from my shoulders all the way down to my toes, caused the buzzing noise!*

At that moment, *I didn't know if I was dead or alive.* So I paused and placed my hands on my knees and pinched my knees with my fingers. I could feel my hands pinching my knees. Then I knew that I was alive! I knew that I wasn't asleep or in a dream; I was awake, it was real.

Then, the other two pilgrims prayed out loud for me, and our assistant table leader prayed out loud and asked The Holy Spirit to cover me from head to foot.

Then, The Holy Spirit wrapped Himself around me from my head to my feet. *Outside of my body, I could see that I was in a large, dark brown cocoon. Inside, it felt like soft cotton.* Although words can't completely describe my experience, that's the closest description that I can write down.

Then I prayed out loud and finished my prayer. The others took their turns praying, and all of us went to bed.

Early the next morning, I was still thinking about the previous night. I was pondering if it really happened. I immediately went down to our table of Matthew, and soon the other two pilgrims joined me. I asked the other two guys if they felt any electricity going through their body last night. Both of them said that they did! I then knew that it wasn't a dream - it was real. I was changed for the rest of my life.

From that moment on, my life changed 180 degrees. No longer was I only working for myself and my family. Now, I'm focused on following Jesus Christ. Even though I receive my paycheck from my employer, I'm now a servant of Jesus Christ and working for Him!!

Reenactment of laying of hands at the Walk to Emmaus Weekend where I was baptized in The Holy Spirit.

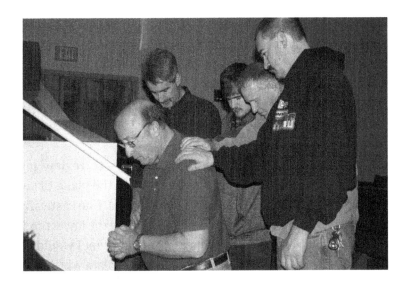

On Sunday evening, after closing ceremonies of the Walk to Emmaus, Nancy and our sponsors Bill and Marilyn picked me up. I felt like a new man living in a new dimension. The spiritual world seems more real than this world. Nancy noticed that I was completely changed.

Rather than watching television or reading the newspaper, I read The Holy Bible both in the morning and in the evening. I watched television evangelists, instead of secular shows, to learn more about following Jesus. Sometimes, I agree with the television evangelists, and sometimes I don't. I compare what I hear on television with The Holy Bible. If what the evangelist said agrees with The Holy Bible, then I learn from them. If not, then I switch to a different television channel.

I was scheduled to fly out the next Saturday morning to go to a Miami business conference. To take advantage of reduced airfares, I reserved plane tickets and hotel reservation for Saturday. The Saturday airfare was $ 300 cheaper than flying on Sunday, and those cost savings would more than offset the extra night in the hotel.

In Nebraska, men attend the Walk to Emmaus Thursday evening to Sunday evening, and the women attend the following week. I knew that Nancy would start her Walk to Emmaus on Thursday night, and experience the wonderful candlelight ceremony on Saturday night, while I was in Miami. I wanted to be at the candlelight ceremony in the worst way. This consumed most of my thoughts for several days.

On Friday evening, I opened my envelope to review my airline itinerary, and I noticed that the date on the plane ticket was Sunday - not Saturday! *The date had changed!* I sarcastically thought great, since work demanded that we use the lowest cost transportation to attend conferences. I thought that I would be in trouble at work or at the very least have to explain why I used the higher cost of airplane travel.

Then I looked closely at the cost of the Sunday airplane ticket, and the *rate was about the same as the Saturday airfare! Now I knew Jesus could do anything.* He can change airplane tickets, including the cost.

Therefore, I had the wonderful experience of attending Nancy's candlelight ceremony on Saturday night to her complete surprise!! She couldn't believe that I was there, rather than in Miami.

After our wonderful Walk to Emmaus experience, I transformed into a new and different person. Previously, I was an angry man until Jesus became my Lord and Savior. Prior to baptism in The Holy Spirit, it was normal for me to be angry about other people and events in my life. I'm no longer the same person that I used to be. My anger has left, and I'm a more pleasant man to be around, plus I now have patience most of the time. Also, drinking beer became a thing of the past.

I also learned to compare what you hear on Sunday morning to The Holy Bible. If the preacher or teacher is basing his/her sermon on scripture, then it's trustworthy. If the preacher adds to or subtracts from The Holy Bible, talk to the minister. If nothing changes, look for a different church.

I saw life differently. *It felt like the scales on my eyes had fallen to the floor.* Now as I <u>slowly</u> read The Holy Bible, the rich words in scripture gradually soak into my mind and heart. Sometimes I ask The Holy Spirit to teach me the meaning of scripture. It's so much fun to read The Holy Bible.

Shortly afterwards, *I felt this tingling sensation throughout my body; the Holy Spirit was revealing to me that The Holy Bible is true!!* This tingling sensation throughout my body along with revealing that The Holy Bible is true, occurred the next day, and then the following day for a total of three days in a row!!

At the time, I felt like "OK, I get the point that The Holy Bible is completely true", but then years later, I realized how important it is to know that The Holy Bible is 100%, completely true. There are some Christians who believe that part of The Holy Bible is true, or others who try to rationalize what they don't understand in The Holy Bible.

Even though I don't understand 100% of everything in The Holy Bible, I know that I know that it's true, because the Holy Spirit revealed that to me plus my faith in God's Word. That brings such a level of peace and comfort to me.

Reading The Holy Bible is so exciting that I can't wait to read it to learn more! It's not a book; books are dead, but *The Holy Bible is alive!* If you read it slowly, it will change you from the inside out. I'm starting to understand it better.

While in the Holy Spirit, I feel this unbelievable joy and my hair stands straight up on my body for about twenty-four hours. *I love and long for that closeness with Jesus and that incredible tingling sensation throughout my body.* I hope that Heaven is like that all the time.

I tried to extend that tingling sensation beyond twenty-four hours, but I have not been successful. After twenty-four hours of that tingling sensation, I broke down and cried knowing that I was not pure. Nancy asked me why I was crying. I told her, and she said not to worry that it was OK. Perhaps, she was right.

Looking back, I realize that it's not something that I'm in control of that result in the Holy Spirit coming to me. It's totally up to The Wonderful Holy Spirit, and I treasure each and every moment with The Holy Spirit.

One time, while reading The Holy Bible, The Holy Spirit transported me to the place, where it was comparable to sitting in a front row seat of a live event. I saw three men in Middle Eastern clothing standing close to a large boulder saying the same words written in scripture.

Interestingly, I felt that it was more exciting to let my mind and heart visualize the written verses, rather than watch it while in the Holy Spirit. I know that this sounds crazy. Then the vision ended.

When I openly talk about The Holy Spirit, some people have asked me about praying in tongues. I feel more comfortable praying in English than in tongues, but I feel the urge to pray in tongues when I'm alone with God, and should pray in tongues more often.

My prayer life also changed after attending The Walk to Emmaus. I start every morning by praying to my Father, Jesus, and the Holy Spirit.

Most of my visions seem to occur after I lay down in my bed, but before I'm asleep. There's no TV, computers, cell phones, etc. at night – it's quiet, just God and me, and God has my complete attention. During this time, The Holy Spirit will teach me about the topic for the next evening's Bible Study, or how to handle certain situations that I'm facing, etc.

After attending the Walk to Emmaus, I now realize that I was baptized in The Holy Spirit. Then I started to be blessed with miracles, finding out my purpose on earth, frequent spiritual events, visions with Jesus, and I started to rely on Jesus and The Holy Spirit. Baptism in The Holy Spirit is described in Acts 8: 14-17

> [14] Now when the apostles who were at Jerusalem heard that Samaria had received the word of God, they sent Peter and John to them, [15] who, when they had come down, prayed for them that they might receive the Holy Spirit. [16] For as yet He had fallen upon none of them. They had only been baptized in the name of the Lord Jesus. [17] Then they laid hands on them, and they received The Holy Spirit.

Here's how I view these scriptures:

- Verse 14 - they received the word of God. Faith comes from hearing the Word.
- Verse 16 – water baptism.
- Verses 15 and 17 – baptized into The Holy Spirit
  - Verse 15 - prayed to receive The Holy Spirit.
  - Verse 17 – Laid hands on them, and they received The Holy Spirit.

If you have only been baptized in water, I strongly encourage you to be baptized in The Holy Spirit. Ask your minister or a spirit-filled person to baptize you in The Holy Spirit.

What wonderful experiences have you had with God? Have you heard His voice? Why don't you tell others about your spiritual experiences? It's lots of fun to do, and they may share their experiences with you also. If God hasn't come to them, encourage them to seek Jesus in their heart.

After experiencing The Holy Spirit in an unbelievable way, our house was attacked by a soldier of Satan soldier, while my wife was inside the house.

Attack by Satan's Soldier

After Nancy's candlelight ceremony on Saturday night, I flew out to Miami for a business conference that lasted most of the week. Bill and Marilyn picked up Nancy on Sunday evening, after the closing ceremonies of her Walk to Emmaus.

I called Nancy that evening, and she told me about her wonderful experiences at her Walk to Emmaus, and I told her how I was able to attend her Saturday evening candlelight ceremony (it was all due to Jesus), and fly out to Miami on Sunday. She was at our home, while I was in my motel room in Miami.

On Tuesday afternoon, I was listening to several speakers in a large conference room. Then to my surprise, security at the Miami conference somehow located me with several hundred people and asked me to follow them. Security startled me when they said to immediately call home because of an emergency. I called Nancy, while she was sobbing through her tears, told me that our house was broken into while she was inside the house! It occurred Tuesday about 3:00 p.m.

I believe that it was no accident that we were attacked after having such unbelievable spiritual experiences. It seems like Satan had sent one of his soldiers into our house to attack Nancy and steal my rifle, shotguns, and shells.

Nancy's office was in our finished basement of our walk-out ranch house. She felt tired, so she went upstairs to take an afternoon nap. As she slept, the intruder tried to smashed open the basement door by ramming a metal cylinder into the center part of the six-panel door. He was unsuccessful. But our basement door had decorative, glass in the upper part of the door. So he smashed the glass in the upper part of the door, he reached down and unlocked the deadbolt lock, cutting his hand on the broken glass and dripping blood on the carpet floor.

He opened the door, walked in, broke the gun cabinet door open and proceeded to spread my shotguns, rifle, and shells across the floor. Nancy was startled and jumped up from the bed, when she heard the loud crash of the metal cylinder crashing into the door and the breaking of glass in the basement. She quickly grabbed her cell phone out of her purse, and ran as fast as she could to our driveway to call 911. Even though she doesn't remember leaving the house, The Holy Spirit took Nancy out of the house just in time.

In the basement, the intruder heard Nancy's footsteps across the floor above, so he quickly ran upstairs, opened the front door with his bloody hand, and peered outside. He saw Nancy calling 911 in the driveway.

He left his bloody fingerprints on the front door, while he quickly grabbed Nancy's purse, ran downstairs and out the basement door leaving the shotguns, rifle, and shells on the basement floor.

He ran down the street behind our house and joined his friends who were waiting for him in a car. Later, we learned from a Council Bluffs detective, which is adjacent to Omaha, that the intruder was on drugs, and that he wanted my shotguns, rifle, and shells. This group of drug users lived in a new, unoccupied house for sale in West Omaha, which is a newer area of the city with more expensive homes, etc.

The previous day, he held a sawed-off shotgun to a guy's head to steal a used play station 2, which was worth about $ 35 at the time. I knew that Satan had control of his heart. When you use drugs and/or alcohol, it dulls your senses and allows evil spirits to enter into your mind and heart. These evil spirits try to gain control of your mind to kill you spiritually first, and then kill you physically.

Within a few days, the police found Nancy's purse (all of the cash was missing), keys, and credit cards.

This reminds me of John 10:10:

> The thief does not come except to steal, and to kill, and to destroy. I have come that they may have life, and that they may have *it* more abundantly.

After the home invasion, the TV news media arrived to report the rash of recent burglaries, and Nancy gave her testimony on television of the Holy Spirit saving her.

Later, Nancy was subpoenaed to attend his court hearing, and testify as to what happened. His court hearing was brief, and Nancy did not have to testify.

I asked for prayers for the intruder at church on the following Sunday to have Jesus cleanse and heal his heart. I wanted to give him a Holy Bible, but the police caught him and put him in jail. It just seems like I never made the time to try to give him a Holy Bible.

I learned that whenever:

- You accept Jesus as your Lord and Savior or experience a spiritual revival or
- You start a new ministry for Jesus or
- Join a team that will bring others to Jesus,

You will likely experience an attack from Satan or one of his demons. Satan's soldier attacked the one person that I loved and valued more than anyone else – my wife Nancy.

Remember that after Jesus was baptized in the Holy Spirit, the Holy Spirit led Him into the wilderness for forty days where Satan tempted Him three times.

> Matthew 3:16-4:2. When He had been baptized, Jesus came up immediately from the water; and behold, the heavens were opened to Him, and He saw the Spirit of God descending like a dove and alighting upon Him. And suddenly a voice *came* from heaven, saying, 'This is My beloved Son, in whom I am well pleased.' Then Jesus was led up by the Spirit into the wilderness to be tempted by the devil. And when He had fasted forty days and forty nights, afterward He was hungry.

I have witnessed attacks by Satan's demons just before or after a spiritual experience a number of times. One seminary student heard a voice in his head regarding his children that did not line up with The Holy Bible. Team members of KAIROS prison ministry or Walk to Emmaus suddenly receive conflicts in their work schedule shortly before they start a weekend.

Another example was a disruption at a Bible Study with the homeless. One guy said he had just talked to Lucifer and needed to disrupt our meeting. We explained that it was a Christian Bible Study and showed him the door.

A Muslim woman wanted to question our faith, but I testified that I had seen Jesus several times, was baptized in the Holy Spirit, etc. At the Des Moines homeless shelter, the projector suddenly stopped in the middle of the DVD "The Star of Bethlehem", and another time the intercom system didn't work, and no one heard the announcement about the Bible Study that night.

After all of these attacks, I learned to frequently lean on The Holy Spirit, who will drive out evil spirits, help me in times of need, and bring others to hear the Word.

I experienced a number of frequent spiritual events that occurred sometimes daily or at least several times a week. It's a wonderful, different way of living.

I learned to lean on The Holy Spirit when facing decisions, such as looking for work and where to live.

Write Down Your Thoughts, Notes, and Comments Here

Part Two:
The Holy Spirit Leads Us and Divine Inspiration

He who has My commandments and keeps them, it is he who loves Me. And he who loves Me will be loved by My Father, and I will love him and manifest Myself to him.

John 14:21

Holy Spirit Guiding Us to Minnesota

Shortly after baptism in the Holy Spirit and the subsequent home invasion, I found out that the company that I had been working for had been sold. At a large meeting, the speaker told the corporate staff that we had six months to find a new job. As long as we completed our work, we were allowed to look for open positions at our desk, call employers, and interview.

At my age, in my fifties, I had some doubts, so I updated my resume and sent out my resume via the Internet to over one hundred companies with open positions. The first week went by, and it was quiet - no postcards, no responses, and no telephone calls. The second week went by and still no responses positively or negatively. Then, the third week and still no responses. I continued to apply for open positions via the Internet. I nervously told Nancy, my wife, that maybe I was too old; maybe no one wanted me.

After three weeks without any responses, I walked into my boss's office and told him that I had a feeling that I would be out of there in thirty days with a job offer. I said that I didn't have any basis for this – just a feeling. Wil said "Great, I hope that it works out for you". *What I didn't know was that Nancy had been fasting and praying all day for a job offer!*

The very next morning (Tuesday), my telephone at work lit up! I started to receive telephone call after telephone call from employers. I knew that it wasn't due to anything that I had done, and that it wasn't a coincidence. *It was Jesus or the Holy Spirit!*

After answering all these telephone calls, my calendar became so full with interviews, that I quit applying for jobs. There were seven companies that were at different stages of making me a job offer. In the past, I would always accept the job offer that paid the most or offered me the most responsibility. This time, I decided to select the job offers differently. My plan was to gather all of the job offers, pray to the Holy Spirit, and then ask the Holy Spirit to pick out which job offer that I should take. That was my plan – not God's plan.

The first offer was a Chief Financial Officer (CFO) position. It was a great job offer, and I always wanted to be a CFO. Therefore, *Nancy and I got on our knees and prayed together on our bedspread, but the response I received that night was extremely negative – anything that could possibly go wrong was in the vision, and I didn't sleep at all that night! I called the headhunter the next morning and politely told her that I decided to turn down the job offer.* I didn't have any other firm offers in hand. Of course, the Chief Executive Officer (CEO) and the recruiting firm wanted to know why. I should have told them the truth, but I didn't. I said that the pay wasn't enough, and that I felt that I couldn't have the impact in the firm that I would like to have. I didn't want to tell them that I prayed about it and received a negative response.

It's fun to chase jobs and know that other people want you and believe in you. Then shortly after this, a large, food manufacturer in Minnesota made me an offer. Since it was the lowest level position and the lowest paying position of the seven possible offers, I kept putting this job offer off while chasing other job opportunities.

Nancy and I traveled to Kansas for a management position in an insurance/investment business. I met their management staff, answered their questions, and asked my questions. While I spent the entire day with their management staff, a real estate agent showed Nancy homes in the area.

But after taking this trip, then the food manufacturer called back with a higher level job and more money. After negotiating the pay and benefits, Nancy and I prayed together to the Holy Spirit and asked Him whether to take this job offer or not. The response to the prayer was very positive – *we both received a vision of a quiet, serene scene in a meadow with a stream in the middle with beautiful music.*

The next morning, I accepted the job offer. The recruiter was completely surprised, since she knew that I had been putting them off. I started there four months after my baptism in the Holy Spirit.

We started to plan on our move to Minnesota, looking at homes for sale, and selling our house in Omaha.

I learned that if God wants you to move, say YES!

If you are unemployed, don't worry about it, fast and pray earnestly and fervently while you apply to numerous open positions in different states.

Sometimes, God may want you to move, perhaps to use you as a vessel somewhere else. I have known of other Christian brothers, who experienced unemployment and just stayed where they were. After a couple of years of unemployment, I advised a close Christian friend that perhaps God wanted him to move. After he prayed and accepted a position in another state, God used him to help another KAIROS prison ministry team, in addition to the previous one that he was a leader.

About five years later, I wondered if those other six jobs still existed. I contacted the other companies and learned that none, zero, of the other positions existed. Only God knows what the future holds for us, and He always picks what is best for us, if we will listen.

After following the guidance of The Holy Spirt for my next job, we needed to move to Minnesota.

Holy Spirit Opens Doors

We placed our house in Omaha on the market at a time when the market was saturated with homes. Also, fall is not the best time of the year to sell a house – holidays fast approaching, weather turning cold, and kids in school. Families don't usually buy or sell homes at that time of the year.

I wanted to set the price above the recommended price of our agent. Even with the higher price, it sold very quickly – about ten days on the market! Then Nancy's job was eliminated. Our long-hair, blue Angolan cat, which Nancy raised from a kitten and loved very much, was very old and had to be put asleep.

So many changes were occurring so fast – too fast for Nancy! Nancy was being uprooted out of her dream home, her life at the country club where she was one of the better women golfers there, comfortable life, and many long-time friends at our church. Her identity would be changing also, since she was highly successful, nationally respected for her professional skills in her industry, and now she would be losing her career, dream house, many friends, long-time pet, and her own view of herself. This move was difficult for her.

I was living in a motel in Minnesota, while Nancy stayed in Omaha tying up loose ends. During those two months, we couldn't find any affordable houses for sale that we liked in Minnesota. We decided to rent while we looked at homes for sale.

Nancy also couldn't find any available apartments! She just broke down and cried. I tried to comfort her, and I told her that the only thing that I knew to do was to pray. We knelt down on the floor and prayed together with our hands clasped together on the bedspread. We prayed for an apartment. The next morning, Nancy drove back to Omaha, while I read the newspaper and found six great units that were advertised for rent that morning!

After visiting six apartments, I picked the one that I liked, and was large enough to hold our furniture from our house in Omaha. Although Nancy was skeptical, she liked it after she saw it. We moved our belongings into the two-bedroom apartment.

At this point, I really didn't understand why the Holy Spirit wanted us to move to Minnesota. I just knew that God knew my future better than I, and it was in my best interest just to *say YES to God and joyfully go with it.*

While we rented the apartment, we decided to design and build a new house in Minnesota. Nancy had cried so much and was devastated by the move, that I felt her spirit would be lifted by building a new house on a lake. But I also felt The Holy Spirit was trying to tell me not to do this, but I didn't know why He was advising me not to build a new house. I made the mistake of ignoring The Holy Spirit. Later, it became very clear. We moved into our new house one year later in the fall of 2006.

Shortly after I was baptized in the Holy Spirit, *The Holy Spirit encouraged me to ask for anything that I wanted.* I thought of Solomon and his tremendous knowledge and wisdom. So, *I asked for knowledge and wisdom.* I didn't feel anything different after asking for knowledge and wisdom, and I soon forgot about it.

Then, roughly two years later, I was curious about a prayer session on Sunday mornings at a church, just a couple of blocks from our new house. The prayer session was held in a room with a few steps leading up to an altar, where about ten people were praying out loud, some in tongues, and some prayed silently. I prayed, as I normally do, in English.

The air in the room seemed to be almost like a thin cloud and thick with the Holy Spirit. I, started praying silently while sitting on the steps to the altar. Then, a man approached me, who was praying in The Holy Bible, and *The Holy Spirit drew him to Daniel 1:17b and the Holy Spirit brought him to me. This man read to me the verse and told me that this verse referred to me.*

> God gave them knowledge and skill in all literature and wisdom;

As I have aged, I have noticed that the Holy Spirit has given me knowledge to understand the spiritual intent of others, and, at times, the wisdom what to say or do. One example is a woman, who was an educational minister and peer of mine at work, who had told some blatant, outlandish lies about me. I perceived that she had a lying spirit within her, and it was strong and quite large.

After I prayed three times to the Holy Spirit seeking guidance, my prayer partner at work came to my cubicle and started talking about this same woman, and how another guy had sued her for vicious lies and won the lawsuit. I decided not to sue her, since her lies were not adversely affecting me at work. This lying spirit was ruining her relationships with others.

God loves music, and even though I don't have a good voice, I love music also. Have you ever heard loud Christian music in the middle of the night that blasted you out of bed?

Wonderful Choir in Heaven

In August 2006, in the middle of the night, roughly 3:00 am, while we still lived in the apartment, I woke up to some very loud Christian music. I wondered who was playing the very loud, religious songs in the middle of the night. I rose up out of bed and looked for a boom box, but I did not find any boom boxes.

But then I looked to my left and noticed that Nancy was sound asleep! Then, I knew that I was the only one hearing it, and I was in The Holy Spirit. *What I heard was a loud chorus of many thousands singing beautiful praises to Jesus.* These words were the same ones that John heard and wrote in The Holy Bible. See Revelation 5:11-13.

> Then I looked and heard the voice of many angels, numbering thousands upon thousands, and ten thousand times ten thousand. They encircled the throne and the living creatures and the elders. In a loud voice they were saying:
>
> "Worthy is the Lamb, who was slain,
> to receive power and wealth and wisdom and strength and honor and glory and praise!"
>
> Then I heard every creature in heaven and on earth and under the earth and on the sea, and all that is in them, saying:

"To him who sits on the throne and to the Lamb
be praise and honor and glory and power,
for ever and ever!

It was beautiful music from a huge choir - many thousands, with such rich and thoroughly perfect music! For the next several weeks, I would hum this music during the day at work, or play it over and over in my head. I was filled with joy.

Others in the workplace thought it was strange that I was smiling so much and humming music, while work was piled on me. I asked Pastor Jim, if he had ever heard a chorus sing during the night. He said no; that I had been given a gift.

Looking back, I'm not sure why it occurred, but this chorus may have been connected to, and perhaps setting the stage for Jesus to come to me soon.

Jesus Takes Me Flying

After moving into our new home, we planned our first train trip to visit our son in the Seattle area. In late September, we rode the Amtrak train from St. Cloud, Minnesota to Seattle to see him. Trains are a great way to travel. Trains force me to relax, food is outstanding, and we meet new friends.

We drove north to St. Cloud, Minnesota, and arrived shortly before midnight, only to find the train depot empty in a deserted, run-down area, but with lights on inside the building. We arrived early, and were the only ones in the building. Then a few others slowly drifted in, and finally the guy taking the tickets arrived at the train depot. We gave him our train tickets and carried our own luggage onto the train, where we located our sleeping room in the dark.

We soon fell asleep in our sleeping room, and awoke the next morning to the gentile rocking of the train hungry for breakfast. After cleaning up and changing clothes, we walked down to the dining car to experience the great food prepared by our on-board chef, ate breakfast with some pleasant people, and later enjoyed the stunning views of Glacier National Park, all of which resulted in a very enjoyable trip.

Our son met us at the ferry landing in Seattle, where we loaded our luggage, sat down and enjoyed the relatively smooth trip across Puget Sound to the Olympic Peninsula. Then he drove us to his house, which has a great view of Hood Canal and the Olympic Mountains.

He also drove us to a small, Norwegian town nearby, where we looked at the little retail shops. I noticed a bag lady going through the garbage cans in the alley. I thought that I should help her, but I continued to shop. When I turned around and walked back to the alley to help her, I discovered that she was gone. I should have immediately gone over to help her, and that bothered me that I did not. My perspective of others in need had changed. I then knew that I should help them.

On our return trip to Minnesota on the train, I didn't sleep well. I was very tired when we arrived at our home, and I could not sleep.

As I was lying on the bed and before I was asleep, **Jesus took me flying into the dark sky.** It was great to be flying with Jesus! He was slightly above me, and I was by His side as we flew into the dark sky. This is depicted on the book's cover.

I was struck with His unbelievable purity, and His brightness in the dark sky. I also discovered that communication with Jesus was different. As soon as I would think of a question to ask Jesus, His response was immediately in my mind. There weren't any verbal words - only my thoughts and His thoughts in my mind.

But His response demonstrated wisdom beyond anything that I could describe. In fact, I don't remember my question or His response, only the immense wisdom and scope of His answers. I was so in awe that everything else didn't matter.

Then I wanted to see the events that will occur during the end of the age. I have been fascinated with this topic in The Holy Bible. I saw horrific storms, it was dark, and the extremely strong winds were bending trees down close to the ground. But then Jesus said that this wasn't about the end of the age. The vision of the storms stopped. I assumed that it was about the lack of purity in my heart.

Then I looked down and saw the earth thousands of miles below. I wanted to see the earth better, so I peered closer and saw a long, line of people on the face of the earth. I looked closer, and I recognized some of the faces. They were individuals who I had made judgmental comments. I noticed that they were shielding their heads and looking up at Jesus. Jesus said that these were His children.

At the time, I felt shame at not having a pure heart, and that I needed to love everyone, but later Jesus would reveal to me that He was showing me that He is the light in this dark world, and that He is the way out of this dark world. Jesus said in John 8:12:

> Then Jesus spoke to them again, saying, "I am the light of the world. He who follows Me shall not walk in darkness, but have the light of life.

Then I saw translucent beings (similar to upright, translucent globules with faces but no arms and no legs) with faces of my Friday morning Emmaus accountability group. They moved around and went into/inside each other and back out. I saw myself, then I looked for Nancy, but I did not see her! I was worried, because I couldn't find Nancy among the translucent beings. *But then I noticed that she and I were one!* She was inside my translucent body. Now, I have a better idea of what it means to be joined together as one.

Then I fell into a deep sleep. I was very excited the next morning!! The unbelievable joy from the tingling sensation throughout my body stayed with me for about a day. It's better than sex, drugs, or anything else on this earth. I wanted the incredible tingling sensation to last longer. I longed for that unbelievable feeling of pure joy and bliss! This longing reminds me of David in Psalm 63:1.

> You, God, are my God,
> earnestly I seek you;
> I thirst for you,
> my whole being longs for you,
> in a dry and parched land
> where there is no water.

I felt so humble and somewhat afraid of the immense power of Jesus. Shortly after this, I experienced Jesus at an unusual place – a funeral.

Jesus' Robe

When the father of a friend passed away, Nancy and I attended his visitation service. We arrived there just in time; only five minutes before it was going to begin. Since it was a full house, we did not have time to view the body in the casket. There were only three to four empty seats in the back row. So, we sat down, and strained our necks and eyes to see over everyone's heads and shoulders to see the casket.

As I watched and listened to the minister, I noticed that there appeared to be an electrical field above the casket. The air above the casket was wavy. I continued to watch the wavy lines in the air above the casket, and it began to move and become more powerful.

Then, suddenly a form of a man, in a bluish-gray haze, appeared on the chair right next to me, as I wondered if the wavy lines were the Holy Spirit. I'm not sure if he was the Holy Spirit or an angel, since I didn't ask him. He answered the question that was in my mind, and said that it was Jesus!! I was very excited – I was going to see Jesus!

As I intently watched these wavy lines, these lines seemed to be increasing in strength, and they started to move more and take form. It appeared to be the bottom of a very large robe, which was piling up inside the funeral home as Jesus was descending! The robe was starting to fill up the entire room. This reminded me of Isaiah 6:1:

In the year that King Uzziah died, I saw the Lord sitting on a throne, high and lifted up, and the train of His *robe* filled the temple.

The power of Jesus was more than I could endure. This force field blew me out of my chair, and as I flew down onto the floor, I caught myself with both hands on the floor so that I wouldn't make a lot of noise and disturb the service. Then the Holy Spirit or angel, in a bluish-gray form, vanished.

Because the power was so intense, I had to turn my head away, which broke off the force field. I felt weak and felt like crawling on the floor, but I edged my way back up into the chair.

After the conclusion of the visitation service, I walked over to my Emmaus friend, whose father had passed away, and excitedly told him about my experience with Jesus. It was exciting, and I was filled with unbelievable joy. When I drove home that evening, I felt so humble and somewhat afraid. Jesus is unbelievably powerful. No human being could stand in His presence unless He wants you to stand in His presence.

After experiencing the power of Jesus at a funeral visitation service, changes were occurring at our church.

Jesus Writes My Purpose on My Heart

Several people, including the Treasurer of our church, had moved to other towns, due to job changes. Our pastor had approached me about accepting the responsibilities of church treasurer, since I have a professional background in corporate finance and accounting.

I really don't enjoy the duties of church Treasurer, since I have previously been the church Treasurer at a different church, and I soon knew more than I really wanted to know, such as who ~~gives~~ returns the most. You cannot give what doesn't belong to you – God owns all of your resources. Also, which bills to pay, since that church didn't have enough funds to pay all of the bills. Most church members don't tithe. Plus, church members will tell you who they think isn't worth their salary.

Church Treasurer is pretty much a thankless job, and not appreciated by the congregation. Therefore, I told the pastor that I would need some time to think about it. After putting the pastor off for three months, I finally accepted the position. It's hard for me to say no to pastors.

There were three people on the church finance committee. One woman reconciled the donated funds, one young man stored and filed tax returns at his house, I processed/paid the bills and printed out the reports.

Things were not going well on the church finance committee. The state of Minnesota sent the church a letter stating that there were problems with what had been filed, and the young man wanted to handle the situation, without anyone else examining the records in question. He refused to let me or anyone else review the records.

I was consumed with this problem, and it drove me nuts. I now know that not forgiving others will eat you up, but I didn't know that I needed to forgive him. I became vocal about this problem with my brothers and sisters in Christ at the Friday morning Emmaus accountability group; which resulted in my tongue spewing anger and venom.

That evening, Nancy and I attended a Bible Study group at the house of a Christian friend. We sat in a semi-circle watching a DVD regarding prophecy. As I watched this DVD, *the Holy Spirit created this tingling sensation throughout my body and cleansed/ healed my heart!*

I felt so much at peace – no anger; just love in this spiritual dimension. I was overjoyed! At the end of the evening, the group stood in a circle and everyone grabbed the next person's hand and prayed. I was the only person who knelt down to pray, since The Holy Spirit had taught me to pray on my knees. Each of us prayed out loud.

I joyfully thanked The Holy Spirit for healing my heart. Since I was in the Spirit, I could see inside my body. I saw something that was very small, but it was growing larger. Also, there was this "silence" in my head increasing in intensity. It felt like my head would soon be bursting wide open.

I knew that I had to do or say something quickly! As the silence intensified in my head, and the item increased in size, so that I could see on my heart written "*homeless shelter*". It was written in perfect cursive. Jesus had written "homeless shelter" on my heart.

I responded that I would be obedient. Then the pressure in my head completely disappeared. Everyone else in the room only heard that I would be obedient, but they didn't know what it was about.

I made the commitment that night to be obedient and to start a homeless shelter. I didn't know anything about homeless people. I also didn't know that the some of the churches in southwestern Minnesota had previously prayed for a homeless shelter, since there are no homeless shelters in that part of the state. Later, I learned that there are homeless people in rural America, as well as in the cities. In fact, some of the homeless people in small towns, farms, and ranches travel to the cities, since that's where most of the homeless shelters are located.

The wonderful news is that *I then knew, without any shadow of doubt, what my purpose on earth was*, and that made life so much easier to focus on as a servant for Jesus. Thank you Jesus!

I told Nancy, on the drive home that night, what had happened. She asked me why I said that I would be obedient, since we don't know anything about homeless shelters or homeless people. She was afraid that I had made a commitment to God that we had no idea how to accomplish it. But I was so filled with unbelievable joy, that I wasn't worried, because I knew that Jesus would provide the leadership and resources to make it a reality. I also knew why God brought us to this small town in Minnesota, and more importantly, my purpose in life.

As we arrived home, we talked about the evening, and we slipped under the covers on the bed. As I was lying in bed before I went asleep, *I could physically feel the Holy Spirit coming into my body. It felt different having someone else inside my body, but I could tell that the Holy Spirit was satisfied, and I fell into a deep sleep.*

I knew that I would devote most of my spare time outside of my job to this project. Therefore, I resigned at the next church council meeting as Treasurer of the church. I then passed around a sign-up sheet at my next Rotary meeting to see if anyone else was interested in helping me start a homeless shelter. The sign-up sheet came back with only one name of a psychologist and a suggestion to contact a woman, who is the manager of social services.

I talked with my pastor about my wonderful experience with Jesus when He wrote "homeless shelter" on my heart. He was very excited about starting a homeless shelter, since he had also previously prayed for having a homeless shelter in the town, and he too wanted to be a part of the project team.

My pastor, the social services manager, a co-worker, and a psychologist came to the first meeting at our church. As it turns out, all of them were very excited about starting a homeless shelter, and each of them work with homeless people in the area. God forms a great project team, when the project leader is Jesus!

Then word of this project spread to others who were interested in starting a homeless shelter. The Salvation Army wanted to be involved in the project and might provide some funding! It was easy at first.

Shortly after we discussed the need for publicity, a photography exhibit of homeless people in rural Minnesota was displayed at the local museum. That group gave us written approval to use their slide show, which we used very effectively to touch people's hearts for the homeless. Also, the local newspaper provided ample coverage, as well as front-page coverage of Jesus' project.

Fund raising is always a critical, on-going focus of any sizable non-profit endeavor. I have never attempted to write a grant before. People, who have written grants, told me that I should request $ 80,000 with the hope that we would get $ 50,000, but the foundation representative told me to request $ 150,000 spread over three years. That was fun and amazing, considering that it was my first attempt at writing a grant.

Others sought out grants from their employers' foundations. Then, we had enough money to purchase the land in an area that was zoned correctly for a homeless shelter, and a good start on designing the proposed facility.

I presented the proposed shelter to the Planning Commission, who passed the proposed facility seven to one, but shortly afterwards, the city council voted it down five to two without any discussion.

I was shocked and as I drove home, I cried out to God asking Him why He brought me here to build a homeless shelter, when the city council voted it down, etc., etc. After arriving home, I fell to my knees and was in deep prayer.

The very next morning before 8:00 am, we received two offers of donated land, even though they didn't know that the city council had voted down our proposed site the night before! We accepted the larger piece of land for the homeless shelter, which was much larger than what we needed. I thanked Jesus! He has such wonderful surprises, and He works in unbelievable ways.

Then, as plans were designed and applications for on-going funds were completed, the owner of the largest motel in town contacted us to rent one wing of the motel, since his motel wasn't doing very well financially. Therefore, we didn't have to build a shelter, but Jesus could provide shelter to the homeless at a local motel.

Thinking back, I loved the Walk to Emmaus experience and earnestly sought out the closest Walk to Emmaus Team.

Agape – Bell Ringing

I joined the Walk to Emmaus Team the following year. I worked on the Agape Team, which handles the pleasant surprises for the new attendees at the Walk to Emmaus four-day event, Thursday evening through Sunday evening.

As a member of the Agape Team, I learned how to serve others, which is such a humbling yet wonderful skill to learn. In comparison, Nancy has always been so good at serving others, and now the Holy Spirit taught me how to serve others. Thank you Holy Spirit!

After working at the Walk to Emmaus and arriving home on Sunday evening, I unloaded my pockets onto the bathroom counter top. I removed the metal badge from my shirt, and placed it on the counter top.

When I got up early the next morning to brush my teeth, take a shower, shave, etc., I heard a bell ringing, and thought that it was my cell phone ringing. I wondered why anyone would be calling me this early in the morning. *I noticed that it was the metal badge vibrating very fast on the counter top.*

I looked at it, then it stopped. After two seconds of silence, the metal badge gave me one last ring. *It was like God was saying thank you.*

I told Nancy about the badge vibrating and making this ringing sound, and she told me that it was ringing throughout the night. She also witnessed the metal badge vibrating very fast, when she got up to go to the bathroom in the middle of the night. Fun.

Prayer is such a powerful tool, because Jesus can do anything, as you'll learn next.

Power of Prayer Without Doubt

Many have joked that the weather man has the only job in the world where he can be wrong the majority of the time and still keep his job. Of course, everyone knows that God controls the weather.

It was very dry that summer and quite warm. We were trying to start a lawn for our new house by planting grass seed, and watering the lawn almost every night, but the weeds were growing faster than the new grass.

So, I prayed for rain, and even though no rain was predicted for that day, it rained that afternoon over our house! I watched a small cloud slowly blow in and rain only over my house and the surrounding houses and nowhere else. I thanked the Lord. I was amazed that it happened the same day as when I prayed and only rained on my house and the surrounding houses.

This reminds me what we can ask for in prayer, and if we have no doubt in our heart, it may be done. See Mark 11:22-24 below.

> So Jesus answered and said to them, "Have faith in God. [23] For assuredly, I say to you, whoever says to this mountain, 'Be removed and be cast into the sea,' and does not doubt in his heart, but believes that those things he says will be done, he will have whatever he says. [24] Therefore I say to you, whatever things you ask when you pray, believe that you receive *them,* and you will have *them.*

There were other weather-related blessings from God. During the bitterly cold winter, it was foggy and icy at the same time. Our new home was built in a new subdivision, on a lake. Driving home in the fog, I could barely see in front of the car or see the side of the road, I was forced to drive very slowly because of the fog and ice. It was so nerve wracking. I asked the Holy Spirit to protect the car from driving in the ditch.

Better yet, I asked Jesus to lift the fog. Shortly thereafter, within thirty seconds), the fog lifted and driving was much improved! I thanked Jesus over and over again. The trees glistened with the ice. The trees, grass, and everything else seemed to glow with the glory of the Lord! Everywhere I looked, I could see the glory of Jesus. Wow!

Then on Saturday morning, I drove into town to help with the weekly food distribution to the poor and homeless, in the basement of our church, called "Matthew 25". As I drove on the highway, it was almost a whiteout, I could barely see in front of the car, since it was a blinding, extremely windy, heavy snowfall. I asked Jesus to lift the blinding snow, and He did within a very short time; so, I again thanked Jesus.

The following winter, as I was driving with Nancy in the passenger seat on the interstate going from Minnesota to Omaha to see our kids and grandchildren, the weather conditions deteriorated and the interstate was icy. I noticed that very few cars were on the interstate, and the ones that were on the interstate were driving slower than normal.

As I was driving with Nancy, *something with tremendous force held my right foot down on the gas pedal all the way down to the floor!* I could not budge my foot at all! The tires did not spin on the ice, and we just started to travel faster than the speed limit with icy conditions. I thought that we would roll the car, as a SUV started to slide out of control in the lane to the right of us and ahead of us. The SUV was doing cookies - driving in circles due to the icy road. I steered the car left into the median and just barely missed the SUV, and we drove past the SUV as it continued to slide in circles. The SUV just missed us by what seemed to be one inch.

Nancy was jubilant and said what a good driver I was! It wasn't me, but it certainly saved us from what would have been a bad accident. Although, I didn't see angels, it was apparent to me that an angel had helped us to avoid an automobile accident. I was so thankful.

Also, while we lived in Minnesota, I experienced several other wonderful experiences with God. A wonderful Christian friend, who seemingly has been given the gift of prophesy, purchased some DVD's of speakers at a prophesy conference in Florida. He invited some couples to meet in his basement, to pray together before we would watch the DVD's, discuss, and then end in prayer.

Afterwards, we gathered in a circle holding hands as each of us would pray out loud. As we were praying, the Holy Spirit (or an angel) was behind our circle and knocked my knees out from me. I fell immediately to the floor catching myself with my hand before I hit the floor. My other hand was still grasping the hand of Shirley, who I thought was also going to fall down. Fortunately, she didn't fall, so I prayed out loud on my knees, while everyone else were standing up in the circle. Later, I thought about what happened, and I think that the Holy Spirit was teaching me to pray on my knees or prostate on the ground. It's a way to be humble when you pray. I'm learning, and I just said thanks to the Holy Spirit for teaching me.

At another meeting, we ended the night in a circle with our hands on each other's shoulders and praying out loud. Then we started to sing the song "There's Something About That Name". We swayed back and forth while singing. Nancy started to pull me back and forth and the speed of all of us moving in a circle rapidly increased as if we were in a spiritual frenzy.

Afterwards as we drove home, I asked Nancy why she was pulling me back and forth into a spiritual frenzy. Amazingly, she said that it wasn't her. Apparently, the Holy Spirit or an angel was pulling us back and forth into a spiritual frenzy. That was the first and only time I have experienced anything like that.

The verses above, Mark 11:22-24, also apply to physical healing. Nancy woke up on a Sunday morning, and her vision was blurry. She said that she would probably lie down and miss church. *I prayed for Jesus to heal her eyes and to remove all blurriness and cloudiness, then Nancy got up out of bed, and her vision was perfect!* We thanked Jesus.

Jesus does have compassion for people who are in need. When people are in crisis, miracles from God can occur. Jesus can heal you either through a doctor or directly. If you need help, pray to Jesus for help. Be persistent like a little child, who will keep bugging you until they get what they need. Keep praying until God heals you or rescues you.

See Daniel 10:2-14

who fasted and prayed for three weeks before receiving a response from God, because of Satan's demons resisted the angel.

In those days I, Daniel, was mourning three full weeks. I ate no pleasant food, no meat or wine came into my mouth, nor did I anoint myself at all, till three whole weeks were fulfilled.

Now on the twenty-fourth day of the first month, as I was by the side of the great river, that *is*, the Tigris, I lifted my eyes and looked, and behold, a certain man clothed in linen, whose waist *was* girded with gold of Uphaz! His body *was* like beryl, his face like the appearance of lightning, his eyes like torches of fire, his arms and feet like burnished bronze in color, and the sound of his words like the voice of a multitude.

And I, Daniel, alone saw the vision, for the men who were with me did not see the vision; but a great terror fell upon them, so that they fled to hide themselves. Therefore, I was left alone when I saw this great vision, and no strength remained in me; for my vigor was turned to frailty in me, and I retained no strength. Yet I heard the sound of his words; and while I heard the sound of his words I was in a deep sleep on my face, with my face to the ground. Suddenly, a hand touched me, which made me tremble on my knees and *on* the palms of my hands. And he said to me, "O Daniel, man greatly beloved, understand the words that I speak to you, and stand upright, for I have now been sent to you." While he was speaking this word to me, I stood trembling.

Then he said to me, "Do not fear, Daniel, for from the first day that you set your heart to understand, and to humble yourself before your God, your words were heard; and I have come because of your words. But the prince of the kingdom of Persia withstood me twenty-one days; and behold, Michael, one of the chief princes, came to help me, for I had been left alone there with the kings of Persia. Now I have come to make you understand what will happen to your people in the latter days, for the vision *refers* to *many* days yet *to come.*"

A person, who I know, needed physical healing. She had so much pain in her legs and feet, she could barely walk. So, I prayed consistently, without doubting at all for three months, and then she could walk without pain.

Recently, The Holy Spirit led me to sit by a man at church, whose new-born granddaughter needed three open-heart surgeries. I prayed that night and saw the finger of Jesus touch the baby's heart, who was healed. This is the first and only time that I witnessed God healing someone.

You can pray for healing, as long as you never doubt God, pray with your whole heart, and never quit praying.

Even though we faced trials and tests like everyone else, Jesus always provides for us, as you'll see in the next spiritual experience involving money.

Tithing Tests

During our last summer in Minnesota, a Christian friend sent me an email saying that the Lord had revealed to him that I would be tested. As various situations came up, I thought that I made it through the test OK, but when the real test came, I didn't always have a Christian heart.

The company that I worked for had never had a layoff in the history of the firm. That year, the company had three layoffs, and I was caught up in the third layoff, and I lost my job shortly before Christmas. Then Nancy lost her part-time right after the first of the year. Here we are sitting in a brand-new house and neither of us has a job!

Looking back, I then understood why the Holy Spirit didn't want us to build the new house! With a new house mortgage and unemployment compensation as our only source of income, I knew that we were in deep, financial trouble.

I was deeply worried, so I prayed to Jesus. Even though I did not see Jesus, I felt His presence, and He just said two words: "Don't worry". I was so relieved!

Now I was focused and filled with so much joy and anticipation in my heart. As my weekly unemployment checks came in the mail, I would write a check for 10% of the gross amount, round it up to fully cover the 10% tithe, and then place it into the church offering plate on Sunday morning. That was my financial plan to get out of this financial mess.

When I placed the check into the plate at church on Sunday morning, I was filled with joy and happiness by returning, we can't give what we don't own, since God owns everything, the first 10% of my income! It was fun.

I know that it defies logic, but we paid our house payments on time, as well as the utilities, etc. while being unemployed. We never had to dip into savings, apply for a loan, use credit cards, etc. plus we still went out to eat occasionally. On paper, we should have been $ 3,000 in the hole each and every month! I don't know how Jesus did it, but I sure was thankful. Perhaps, He was changing the numbers in my checking account. In fact, I had more time to work on Jesus' project: a new homeless shelter called The Refuge - A Fresh Start. I worked on the planning activities and board meetings. This went on for five months!

My history of giving to the church goes back to when I was a boy; my mom would give me a nickel to place in the plate on Sunday morning at Sunday school. I would hold my fist, with the nickel in it over the plate, and then drop the nickel into the plate hoping that no one else saw I was only giving five cents. Then, a few years later, my mom gave me a dime; I asked if that was ok, because it was twice as much. She said yes that I could place it in the plate at Sunday school.

Later in life, when I was in my twenties, I would open my wallet and give whatever was in my wallet in the plate at church on Sunday morning, rolling up the dollars into a tight roll, and letting the roll of dollar bills ride high on the plate.

Then, in my thirties, my approach to tithing changed to writing down my after-tax income, list all of our bills, and whatever was left over, I would give to the church. At first, I was giving 1% to the church, the next year I doubled it to 2%, and then we increased it to 3%. The following year, I sweated bullets and gave 5%, but I felt depressed, since I knew that I would never come close to giving 10%. It just seemed to be out of reach for me.

Now I know, that *Jesus is not interested in leftovers!!* I learned that if you thank Jesus as soon as you are paid and <u>immediately</u> write the check for the full 10% of gross income, then Jesus will redeem your other 90%. Plus, you will always have enough money to bring your tithe to your local church and extra funds for offerings to homeless organizations, mission activities, etc.

Jesus will provide for you and protect you if you will trust Him. See Malachi 3:10-12, underling added.

> Bring <u>all the tithes</u> into the storehouse,
> That there may be food in My house,
> And try Me now in this,"
> Says the LORD of hosts,
> "If I will not open for you the windows of heaven
> And <u>pour out for you *such* blessing</u>
> That *there will* not *be room* enough *to receive it.*
>
> "And <u>I will rebuke the devourer</u> for your sakes,
> So that he will not destroy the fruit of your ground,
> Nor shall the vine fail to bear fruit for you in the field,"
> Says the LORD of hosts;
> "And all nations will call you blessed,
> For you will be a delightful land,"
> Says the LORD of hosts.

Pray about it, try it, and see for yourself. The only way tithing works is to put Jesus first in your life, including money. Are you putting Jesus first in your life by tithing to your local church?

While experiencing financial blessings for five months with only unemployment, I learned how others count on Jesus every day in Honduras.

Real Faith in Honduras

While we were unemployed and living in Minnesota, Nancy and I decided to update our passports. As we were updating our passports, the telephone rang. A close Christian friend asked me if I wanted to go on a mission trip to Honduras. One team member cancelled at the last minute, and they called me about the opening. I said yes that I would like to go on the mission trip, and shortly after that telephone conversation, I flew with the team in February to Honduras.

Our team's assignment was to build a wall for a new church in a rural area of Honduras. The new church would be holding their first church service. On Thursday, many Hondurans walked down, up, and over the hills and roads for their first church service. The church was packed, and everyone sang loudly hymns which they knew from their hearts. *You could feel the electricity in the air – the Holy Spirit was there.*

In Honduras, mothers don't know where their food would come from to feed their children. Unemployment is quite high. So, they pray to Jesus. They count on Him for their survival, and He always provides for them. Their faith is very real to them, and what a great lesson for us.

They also asked us to build a bridge over the stream, since they are trapped by the rapidly flowing, deep water in the rainy season. This bridge would allow them to walk to church, go to the closest town to purchase food, talk with others on the other side of the river, etc. Our team included an engineer, a farmer, and others with the right skills to design and build a bridge. I just provided willing hands, back, and feet for manual labor. The bridge was completed, and we flew home.

After several months, I heard that the bridge was still intact without any problems, and no one had fallen into the river. I was happy and comforted, because this was my first and only bridge.

Jesus used our unemployment as an opportunity to use me in the nation's capital, Washington D.C.

Write Down Your Thoughts, Notes, and Comments Here

Part Three:
Letting Your Light Shine
By Doing Good Works

Let your light so shine before men, that
they may see your good works
and glorify your Father in heaven.

Matthew 5:16

Serving the Homeless in
Our Nation's Capital

While we were unemployed in Minnesota, my daily routine was to pray, read my Holy Bible, work on activities for the planned homeless shelter, apply on-line for open positions, and to vary the routine, one time I applied for a few federal government positions. I didn't care where the open positions were located, since Nancy and I were empty nesters. It seemed like I applied for hundreds of open positions.

I received a telephone call in April to set up a job interview for an open position at a federal agency in Washington DC. Since I really didn't remember applying for this job, I enthusiastically talked with the hiring manager, while trying to figure out the responsibilities of this position at the same time. I was overqualified for the position, but they said that I was their top candidate for the position.

While The federal agency made me an offer, I received a better offer, more money, from a corporation in Des Moines, Iowa. After starting work in Des Moines for a couple of days, as a matter of courtesy, I decided to let the manager at the federal agency know that I had accepted another position. He wanted to know how much the corporation was paying me, so I told him. Then the federal manager called me back a few days later with an offer that matched their pay, but the federal benefits and job security were better. I didn't know that you could negotiate with a federal agency. I accepted their offer, and Nancy and I loaded up a U-Haul truck and moved to northern Virginia.

My manager was fantastic, plus two of my peers at work regularly read their Holy Bibles! I had never seen employees reading The Holy Bible at work in private companies. It was so refreshing.

I really don't think that it's an accident that I was hired to work in such a group of Christians. After experiencing so many spiritual events, I now know that there are no coincidences, no such thing as luck, mojo, etc. Everything happens for a reason, although we normally don't know why. Due to angels, the Holy Spirit, demons, all of whom we normally cannot see, they influence our minds and hearts, and then things happen.

I learned later, that it was definitely not normal for federal employees to read The Holy Bible at work either. This was an unusual situation, which I enjoyed. Thank you Jesus for placing me with two other Christians at my work.

At work, I also discovered a group of Christians that met on Wednesdays over lunch for prayer and reading The Holy Bible. They are a great group of Christians. My prayer partner at work suggested that we should start up an outreach mission. So, three of us went to Franklin Park in downtown Washington DC after work and asked the homeless people, who were sitting on the park benches, if they wanted to give their lives to Jesus. Three people accepted that invitation to accept Jesus as their Lord and Savior that afternoon! That was fun!

Later, this wonderful group of three Christians grew in numbers as we provided food, clothing, health kits, love, prayers, on Saturday afternoons to the homeless people that hung out in downtown Washington DC. We learned that other groups came on the first three Saturdays of the month to distribute food, so we changed our food/love/prayer event to the fourth Saturday of the month. Some of the homeless had not eaten at all, until they came through our line in the afternoon.

In planning for our first Saturday event, we didn't know how many sack lunches and bottles of water to bring, so we prepared fifty sack lunches, fifty water bottles, etc. I asked that people pray over the food as they prepared the sack lunches. We always opened up in prayer, distributed the food, clothing, etc., and closed in prayer.

As we set up our table on the sidewalk for the first time, I noticed that the line of homeless people quickly formed down the block and around the corner! *There were well over 150 people in line!* I knew that we didn't have enough food and water bottles, so I thought that we would give out what we had, and some people would be upset or angry. As we prayed and started handing out the food, water, etc., many came through the line and were so grateful.

Then, when the last person in line picked up the last sack lunch and water bottle, I knew that I had witnessed a miracle, and I was part of that miracle! It reminded me of Jesus feeding the 5,000 men, plus families, in Matthew 14:15-21.

> When it was evening, His disciples came to Him, saying, "This is a deserted place, and the hour is already late. Send the multitudes away, that they may go into the villages and buy themselves food."
>
> But Jesus said to them, "They do not need to go away. You give them something to eat."
>
> And they said to Him, "We have here only five loaves and two fish."
>
> He said, "Bring them here to Me." Then He commanded the multitudes to sit down on the grass. And He took the

five loaves and the two fish, and looking up to heaven, He blessed and broke and gave the loaves to the disciples; and the disciples gave to the multitudes. So they all ate and were filled, and they took up twelve baskets full of the fragments that remained. Now those who had eaten were about five thousand men, besides women and children.

It is in the distribution of food that the miracle occurred for the disciples and for us.

So, next month, we prepared 75 sack lunches, water bottles, etc., and later we increased to 100, even though we were usually serving well over 150 homeless people.

I have witnessed this same miracle occur many times. Jesus takes care of the homeless through us, regardless if they have a job or regardless if they believe in Him. It's truly amazing! This occurred every month, with one exception, for roughly four years.

Only one time did we run short of food, water bottles, etc. It was when a volunteer, who agreed to prepare fifty sandwiches, ordered her son to make the sandwiches. He objected to making the sandwiches, and made fewer than fifty sandwiches. It was done with anger and resentment. On that Saturday, we ran short. All of the other months, we had plenty of food, water, etc. for everyone, even though we were serving many more than what we had prepared.

I remember one time, it was winter, and I had brought hot chocolate, hot water, cups, and spoons. I had purchased ten hot chocolate boxes with ten hot chocolate packets in each small box. Therefore, I had a total of 100 hot chocolate packets, spoons, cups, and napkins.

Others were bringing the sandwiches, chips, fruit, clothes, health kits, etc. We opened up in prayer, distributed the food, clothing, etc., and then closed in prayer. That afternoon, many came back for second and third hot chocolate drinks, because of the cold weather. Drinking hot chocolate was a popular item, since we were outside in a park in the winter.

Afterwards, when we were cleaning up, I noticed that I had not opened eight of the ten boxes of hot chocolate! Unbelievable, since we had served well over 200 hot chocolate drinks that day! *It was in the handing out of hot chocolate drinks where the miracle occurred. Jesus is so good.*

We, also, held communion a few times in the park. The homeless in the park loved it, but there were some homeless, who were non-believers and just drank the grape juice and ate the bread, because they were hungry. Also, a volunteer questioned whether we should use an ordained minister rather than me. I wasn't offended, so I asked an ordained minister to conduct communion in the park. Since the volunteers came from different denominations, there were subtle differences in the way to serve communion, so we abandoned serving communion, which disappointed some of the homeless people.

We, also, conducted altar calls several times. There were several people who came forward and accept Jesus as their Savior and Lord. Most of the times that we served food, love, clothes, health kits, homeless people would come forward and ask for prayer.

Without failure, as we are cleaning up, Jesus would always place immense joy in my heart; so much that I couldn't wait for next month to do it again!

Another memorable event was when I was talking to one homeless woman about the miracle of feeding so many with only fifty sack lunches and water bottles. As I was telling her of this miracle, she had that wonderful tingling sensation go throughout her body! Next month, she came back to tell me that she told everyone in the park about her wonderful spiritual experience! What fun!

I have many, fond memories of providing food, clothes, love, prayers, and at times communion and altar calls with the homeless people in downtown Washington D.C. But my most fond memories were at Christmas time. One minister of a church would bring his choir and musicians, in addition to food, clothes, love, health kits, McDonald gift certificates, etc. The musicians and choir members would sing while we were handing out food, love, etc. Afterwards, we would distribute paper copies of Christmas carols, and sing our favorite Christmas songs, while the homeless sang with us. Some of the homeless people had good voices, and it was so much fun and memorable.

Have you seen homeless people sitting in the parks or other areas and just walked by? I recommend that you and at least one other person approach them and get to know them. Perhaps, you can help someone else in this world to know Jesus. Let Jesus' light shine through you to others.

Every fall, usually in November, in the Washington DC downtown park, we held an event that distributed outdoor winter coats, waterproof gloves, stocking caps, hats, sweat shirts, etc. and the crowds were sizable. I requested that the clothes not have any holes, and reminded the church members that we were serving mostly adult men. Church congregations really got behind this event and supported it with donated, most items were newly purchased, winter clothes. Eventually, the event grew in size until it was one of the larger outdoor winter clothing events in in Washington D.C. for the homeless. *It wasn't me – it was Jesus!* Since the homeless valued outdoor, winter clothes more than food, the crowds at times became unruly. It forced us to reorganize the event, so that only about thirty at a time could select what they wanted.

At roughly the same time as the downtown homeless ministry started, someone forwarded an email to me asking if anyone would be interested in leading a Bible Study at the local homeless shelter on Saturday mornings in northern Virginia. There are a number of homeless people who live in tents in the woods, cars, and lean-to's, who walk to this shelter on Saturday mornings to eat breakfast and take a shower. The Bible Study would start at 9:00 am and end 1 – 1.5 hours later.

Even though I had never led a Bible Study before, I felt drawn to help lead this Bible Study, so I responded yes to the email. Fortunately, another guy who knew The Holy Bible and was comfortable in leading the Bible Study also responded yes, so we were the initial leaders of this Bible Study with the homeless. After praying to the Holy Spirit for guidance, I was led to the Book of Acts, which we used to start the Bible Study.

At the first class, only two homeless men attended. We slowly read, digested with cross references, thought about, and discussed the scriptures, letting the wisdom soak into our hearts and minds. This Bible Study brought hope and joy as the size of the Bible Study increased to eight, then to twelve.

The regular attendees called it their church, rather than a Bible Study, and I noticed that sometimes some of the men would remove their hats/caps out of respect for this time with Jesus. Some of the homeless are not welcomed at churches, because they are sex offenders, clothes are dirty, or they reek, since they don't have a shower readily available. I believe that we should welcome everyone to pray with us and to worship Jesus, plus we should help the homeless.

About two months later at the Bible Study, we held our first communion service and tears flowed freely. That was the first time that I had noticed tears flowing freely at communion. I did not notice that at my regular church. That's the Holy Spirit working within their hearts.

Then, we started to form a circle at the end of the Bible Study, lay hands on those who needed healing, and pray out loud for their healing. Several guys said afterwards that they felt something warm in their arms, hands, or feet.

The Holy Spirit blessed not only the homeless people who attended, but also those who were serving them. It was a special time and place. Then, I felt this incredible joy in my heart. Thank you Jesus.

Homeless in Northern Virginia

A state elected representative complained to the state Department of Transportation (DOT) of homeless people sleeping on state property that was too close to the highway. As a result of his complaint, the state DOT and state police forced the homeless to move off state property. The homeless were forced to move to wooded areas that are on private property.

I called the state political representative and was very firm with him telling him to read The Holy Bible. He said that he was a Christian, and I have included Matthew 25:35-36 and

Isaiah 58:7-11 below. I told him what he did was wrong and evil, that he was not accountable to me or anyone else, but he is accountable to God, thanked him for his time, and hung up. The following year, this same state political representative had a changed heart and set up a $ 2M fund for homeless shelters in his area. When you speak up for Jesus, it will have an impact.

See Matthew 25:35-36:

> for I was hungry and you gave Me food; I was thirsty and you gave Me drink; I was a stranger and you took Me in; I *was* naked and you clothed Me; I was sick and you visited Me; I was in prison and you came to Me.'

Also, Isaiah 58:7-11:

> *Is it* not to share your bread with the hungry,
> And that you bring to your house the poor who are cast out;
> When you see the naked, that you cover him,
> And not hide yourself from your own flesh?
> Then your light shall break forth like the morning,
> Your healing shall spring forth speedily,
> And your righteousness shall go before you;
> The glory of the Lord shall be your rear guard.
> Then you shall call, and the Lord will answer;
> You shall cry, and He will say, 'Here I *am*.'
> "If you take away the yoke from your midst,
> The pointing of the finger, and speaking wickedness,
> *If* you extend your soul to the hungry
> And satisfy the afflicted soul,
> Then your light shall dawn in the darkness,
> And your darkness shall *be* as the noonday.

The Lord will guide you continually,
And satisfy your soul in drought,
And strengthen your bones;
You shall be like a watered garden,
And like a spring of water, whose waters do not fail.

I noticed that government representatives and employees in one city government also has forced homeless people to move from place to place using the excuse that one person saw them and complained. Therefore, that city government keeps forcing homeless people, who live in tents, to move from one wooded area to another wooded area. Are the people, who complain about seeing homeless people feeling guilty for not helping the homeless, or is it just hatred of homeless people? I really don't know, but it defies any reasonable sense of logic.

Other people will blame homeless people for mistakes, life style of drinking, etc. without knowing them. Therefore, what is the basis for judgment? We have all made mistakes, and to judge people that you don't know is also wrong. I guess they just like to blame the victim. This type of insane treatment of homeless people is not based on The Holy Bible.

Are some city government people under the influence of evil spirits, or do they think that forcing them to move will cause them to move to another city or state? All of the homeless people are the sons or daughters of someone, and for whatever reason, they cannot go home, or they don't have any relatives in the area to help them. Sometimes, family members are the problem. In despair or boredom, some homeless will drink alcohol or beer or use drugs. Could unforgiveness or judgment of others be a root cause of some homelessness?

I encourage people to get to know homeless people. You can make a difference in their lives by actually doing Matthew 25:35-36 and Isaiah 58:7-11, which are listed above. If you and your spouse like a homeless person, and they agree to your house rules, you can let them stay in your house, they can pay for their portion of the food, they can clean up their room, etc. Don't let fear determine whether you will serve Jesus by serving others. Also, take time to tell them your testimony of Jesus, read The Holy Bible with them, and pray with them. This will also distinguish your efforts from Muslims, Hindu's, etc. In Matthew 4:4, Jesus said:

> But He answered and said, "It is written, 'Man shall not live by bread alone, but by every word that proceeds from the mouth of God.'

I also give money that I have in my wallet to homeless people. I know that some people question how the homeless will use the money, but I view it as the correct thing to do. See Deuteronomy 15:7 – 11 below. I added the underlining.

> If there is among you a poor man of your brethren, within any of the gates in your land which the Lord your God is giving you, you shall not harden your heart nor shut your hand from your poor brother, but you shall open your hand wide to him and willingly lend him sufficient for his need, whatever he needs. Beware lest there be a wicked thought in your heart, saying, 'The seventh year, the year of release, is at hand,' and your eye be evil against your poor brother and you give him nothing, and he cry out to the Lord against you, and it become sin among you. You shall surely give to him, and your heart should not be grieved when you give to him, because for this thing the Lord your God will bless you in all your works and in all to which you put your hand. For the poor will never cease from the

land; therefore I command you, saying, '<u>You shall open your hand wide to your brother, to your poor and your needy, in your land</u>.'

I believe that God has provided some people with more funds than others, so that those with more funds can show His love to others. How the homeless use the money is between them and Jesus, and it's not on you. When homeless people approach me, sometimes I wonder if Jesus has placed that person before me, because He is counting on me to help that person.

I remember one instance of riding the metro, subway in Washington DC area, and I saw an older woman sitting by herself at the back of the subway car with a large, plastic bag of her clothes. I walked up to her and gave her five dollars, tears rolled down her face, and she was so grateful and happy.

A young man who was living in a tent in the Woodbridge, Virginia area asked me if I would help him by giving him a ride to the pawn shop and pay for one month on the laptop that he sold at the pawn shop. I agreed, and learned that he had sold his most valuable possession, his laptop, so that he could buy his kids Christmas presents, while he is living in a tent. Wow.

Another guy wanted me to buy minutes for his cell phone, because he wanted to call his son that day to wish him a happy birthday. His family lives in another state, and he can't leave Virginia until his parole is over.

These experiences are priceless. The police found one young man sleeping on the sidewalk, but he wanted to go home to see his wife and kids, who he hadn't seen in a long time. I gave him a ride to the bus station, and bought him a bus ticket. His wife called me, and she was overfilled with joy! I have helped others to move back home to be with their children. It's so much fun. I tell all of them to thank Jesus, not me, since it's because of Jesus that I help them.

You can be that person that helps someone else reunite with their family and Jesus, that will give them hope and a real future with Christ.

Your testimony of Jesus may help others to take action in helping the homeless, as I learned in Northern Virginia.

Nehemiah House

At a Saturday morning Bible Study sessions with the homeless, I gave my testimony of baptism in The Holy Spirit, since my testimony will inspire others. The room was full, including some who were intently listening in the sleeping area of the homeless shelter. The Holy Spirit used my testimony as an opportunity to touch the hearts of several in the room.

Afterwards as I was leaving, one man asked me why I don't start a homeless shelter there. Even though I actually didn't start a homeless shelter in Minnesota (it was Jesus and I was just following Him), *at that moment, Jesus overfilled my heart with this special joy throughout my body.*

I then knew that it was it was time to get back to work to start a new homeless shelter by forming a 501 ('c) 3 non-profit organization, a Board of Directors with bylaws, incorporate as a non-profit, and then design a new homeless shelter in northern Virginia, the Nehemiah House.

We adopted the name Nehemiah House based on Nehemiah 2:17(b), since this will be a place where Jesus is the focus, and lives will be rebuilt.

> Come, let us rebuild the wall of Jerusalem, and we will no longer be in disgrace.

The Nehemiah House would provide not only shelter and food where Jesus is the center of the organization, but

Jesus would also transform lives. The planning and design is completed. They just need funding to build it and start the operation of it.

The man who asked me about starting a homeless shelter became a good friend and officer of Nehemiah House. The vision of the Nehemiah House is shown below.

Nehemiah House Vision

- *"Restore Dignity, Hope, and Transform lives through skill development and spiritual growth"*
- *50 Rooms with 1 – 2 per Room*
- *Christian Housing*
- *Transformed Lives by Jesus & Holy Spirit*
- *Stable – Safe Environment*
- *Job Training and Job Placement*

On a warm, calm Saturday morning in the fall, the morning Bible Study with the homeless was over, and I drove my old, black 1996 4Runner to a local restaurant to eat lunch. Afterwards, I would be going to Franklin Park in downtown Washington D.C. to hand out food, clothes, love, and prayers to the homeless, who live around that park.

As I walked out to the parking lot and opened the door on this calm day, the door flew open and knocked into my forehead. My eyeglasses flew, and I was in a daze. That was truly a supernatural event, since there wasn't any wind. Surprisingly, everyone inside the restaurant rushed to the windows to watch me! I could see their faces in the window as I was recovering from the sudden, powerful door slamming into my forehead, which knocked off my glasses. That was strange.

After serving the homeless in Franklin Park, I drove home, and I looked in the mirror and noticed that the door left an imprint on my forehead that was similar in shape to the first letter of God's name Yahweh in Hebrew!

This reminded me of God changing Abraham's name to Abraham. See Genesis 17:5:

> No longer shall your name be called Abram, but your name shall be Abraham; for I have made you a father of many nations.

I had recently learned in a Bible Class, that if you use the first letter in God's name and add it to Abram; it changes Abram to Abraham and Sari to Sarah. The imprint on my forehead lasted about three weeks. I didn't tell anyone else about it, since neither Jesus nor the Holy Spirit directly told me why it happened.

I stopped using Dan as my first name, and switched it back to Daniel. Several reasons led me to make this change. One reason is that Daniel is my God-given name. My mother told me that she named me after Daniel in Old Testament. Perhaps, that's why I have such a great interest in the book of Revelation, Daniel, Zechariah, etc.

Another reason is that Dan was the location where idol worship occurred in the Old Testament. Also, in Revelations, chapter seven, the tribe of Dan is not listed in the 144,000 sealed servants.

Therefore, it was easy for me to start using Daniel, rather than Dan, as my name, but it was difficult for my wife, children, etc. to call me Daniel, since they had always known me as Dan.

When I lived in the Washington D.C. area, I used the Metro and learned not to fear anyone.

Attacker Disappears

For my job, I needed to attend a meeting in New Carrollton, Maryland on a Tuesday mid-morning. So, I walked across the street and down to the closest metro station. I noticed a man on the subway platform, who seemed nervous and was watching me. So, I moved down the subway platform to wait before boarding a different metro car. He moved to the same platform as me, and then as the metro cars arrived, I quickly moved to a different car and boarded. At the last second, he also boarded that same metro car. I noticed that there were only about six people on this car, and he was several rows in front of me.

So, I bowed my head, closed my eyes, and prayed for help from the Holy Spirit. *As I raised my head and opened my eyes, he was gone!* The subway car had not stopped, and we were between metro stations, and there was not any sound from the metro doors opening or closing, so he did not go out the door to the next car. I looked underneath the car seats, and he was nowhere to be found.

He was simply gone. I don't know where he went or what happened to him. I just give thanks to the Holy Spirit. I now know that if you hand over all aspects of your life to Jesus and are working for Jesus, that He will protect you and provide for you.

As a servant of Jesus, you don't need to be afraid of anything nor worry about anything. You can live in peace that surpasses all understanding. See Philippians 4:5-7 below.

Let your gentleness be known to all men. The Lord *is* at hand.

Be anxious for nothing, but in everything by prayer and supplication, with thanksgiving, let your requests be made known to God; [7] and the peace of God, which surpasses all understanding, will guard your hearts and minds through Christ Jesus.

Have you surrendered to Jesus, asked Him to come into your heart, asked The Holy Spirit to make the major decisions for you, and live a life without any fear, doubts, worries, or lies? Live a new life where you can smile again, laugh again, and be an ambassador for Jesus. It's a different way of living. See 2 Corinthians 5:20 (a):

Now, then, we are ambassadors for Christ,

Are you an ambassador for Jesus? Have you talked to anyone this week about Jesus? Sometimes, following rules and just living a life of obedience can be difficult. Do you demonstrate your love for Jesus by being obedient to Him?

Many believe in Jesus, but they like to retain control over their life, control over their money, and make their own decisions. It's much better to ask Jesus to take control of your life, ask The Holy Spirit to make the decisions for you. Let Him decide, and you just follow through. Then, you will no longer fear unemployment, crime, thefts, lies, or anything else. What a difference this will make in your perspective, personality, attitude, marriage, job, etc. Life is so much easier, pleasant, and worth-while.

Hopefully, you don't fear anything. Do you? Fear doesn't come from God. Be in prayer and turn your fears over to Jesus.

There are occasions, when Jesus touches a person through a miracle, including bringing someone back to life.

Jesus Brings Grandson Back to Life

Since our move from Minnesota to the Washington DC area, we lived in an apartment. So, we stored most of our stuff that would not fit in our apartment in two, large storage units in Minnesota.

We decided that we no longer needed our stuff in the two storage units. Therefore, Nancy and I drove back to Minnesota to empty our two storage units to avoid paying any more storage fees for several years. We donated our stuff to a local church, and if they didn't want it, we threw it away in a local landfill.

The minister and a member of his church arrived to help us load items that the church wanted or to those in need. After they took some furniture items to the church, they returned again and again to take items to other locations. They made a number of trips, which was so helpful to us. It was a bigger undertaking than either of us had foreseen and without the blessing of those wonderful people, we would have buckled under the strain.

After we cleaned out our storage units and donated most of our stuff to this church, we drove back to northern Virginia. We received a short text message saying that our grandson, age two, had fallen into a swimming pool. There was so much that the text message didn't say, such as we didn't know if the swimming pool was full of water or not. Since we didn't really know exactly what happened, we immediately drove from Minnesota to Omaha.

We then learned that our grandson had actually drowned in the swimming pool!! My son heard the screams of his older son and ran down to the swimming pool. This is a different kind of scream, when you know someone is dying or dead. It's the scream of death. Since he was on the bottom of the swimming pool, blue in color; he was physically dead. My son didn't think that it would do any good, but he gave him CPR anyway. ***Our grandson came back to life**! I know that there is only One that can bring people back to life, and that's Jesus.* Thank you, thank you, thank you Jesus!

We believe we were doubly blessed with the gift of his life. As the members of the family and some relatives gathered for a meal at a restaurant, I prayed out loud and offered a heartfelt prayer of thanksgiving, and some of the relatives told me that the prayer was special, and they felt something in their heart.

Our grandson continued to run around the restaurant laughing and having fun, while not showing any effects from his drowning. He did not have nightmares, recurring dreams of drowning, etc. Amazing!

In the midst of difficulties and tragedy, there are always blessings. Then, we drove back to our home in northern Virginia, where I experienced healing and divine revelation.

Jesus and The Never-Ending Stream/River of Love

That fall, I experienced severe pain on my left side of my back, which moved to the middle of my back and seemed to be increasing in pain and size. It felt different than a pulled muscle, and I was afraid it might be cancer. So, I called the doctor, described the symptoms, and he referred me to a Pulmonologist. It would be two to three weeks before I could get an appointment. The pain continued to increase in severity, until on Saturday night, I could not sleep, and I decided to go to the hospital emergency room immediately after church the next day.

That night, I prayed fervently with my eyes closed, and I saw Jesus in a meadow by a stream. As He walked closer to me, my head merged with His head, my heart merged with His heart, and the rest of my body and soul merged with His body and soul. We became as one, and immediately all of my pain was gone, and I fell instantly into a deep, peaceful sleep! The next morning, we drove to church, and I announced my miraculous healing to the congregation, and many were amazed. The pain never reoccurred.

Three weeks later, as I laid down to sleep, I closed my eyes, and I saw hills, trees and rocks, and they were crying out "Jesus", "Jesus" in a loud voice which echoed all around. This reminded me of Luke 19:40 when Jesus said,

I tell you, He replied, if they keep quiet, the stones will cry out.

I stretched open my mouth as far as I could and shouted along with them. Our voices thundered "Jesus", and echoed in the surrounding hills. The thought came to me that I should open my eyes to see if my shouts of "Jesus" woke up Nancy. She was sound asleep beside me, so I knew that I was in the Spirit.

Therefore, I stretched my mouth wide open, and I continued to yell "Jesus", "Jesus" as loud as I could along with the rocks and trees. I closed my eyes again, and Jesus appeared to me standing by the stream in the meadow as He had appeared in other visions.

He revealed to me that the reason that I am experiencing such dramatic visions is to get my full attention. He also revealed to me that when He took me flying in the darkness, it was to show me that He is the light in this dark world, and that He is the way out of this dark world.

Plus, He revealed to me, that the stream He is standing close to, is *a never-ending stream of love that has no beginning and no end*. He said through thoughts, not words, that many people stand poised on the edge of the bank of the stream, some may tip their toes into the water, but few immerse themselves into the water, because they don't trust Jesus!! I was very sad and wondered why so many don't trust Jesus!

Jesus wants us to trust Him and to immerse ourselves in His stream of never-ending love. I leaned backwards, fell into the stream, instantly the stream increased in size into a river, and I was floating on top of the water face up with my arms and legs spread out in spread-eagle fashion.

Then, a blinding light shone through my body like a projector into the darkness above. I felt this was a message to everyone, not just me, to trust in Jesus, and let His light, not my light, of love shine through you to the rest of the world.

Afterwards, I couldn't wait to tell others about my spiritual experiences. Nancy has told me to wait until new acquaintances become our friends before I would tell them about my spiritual experiences. I don't care if others think I'm a nut. I must tell others my testimony of Jesus and The Holy Spirit; otherwise, my head feels like it would burst wide-open. It's just so much fun, plus Jesus inserts this unbelievable joy in my heart, so I can't wait to tell someone else! As I have told others about some of my experiences, I have been asked how I can remember all of these details without notes. *I explained to them that when these wonderful events occur, they become part of the cells in my body; it's not just a memory in my mind; it's now part of who I am.*

At our church in northern Virginia, we enjoyed a Bible class taught by one my Emmaus friends Bill. At Bill's adult Sunday School Class, I met a great guy who helped me to expand my ministry of helping the homeless.

KAIROS Prison Ministry

I don't believe things just happen, coincidences, or luck, since I know that evil spirits, angels, The Holy Spirit, Jesus, and our Father in Heaven are real and very active. There are reasons why something happens; it's just that we don't always know the reason. So, when someone says something to me that is in alignment with scripture, I listen very carefully, because I don't know if God is speaking through them to me or not.

During Sunday School Class at church, I was approached about joining the KAIROS prison ministry. I remembered Matthew 25:36:

> I *was* naked and you clothed Me; I was sick and you visited Me; I was in prison and you came to Me.'

I decided to join the KAIROS prison ministry. I also knew that some of the homeless were previously incarcerated in prison, and helping the homeless was my purpose on earth. Therefore, it seemed to me that the KAIROS prison ministry would be a good tie-in with my purpose of helping the homeless. I was excited about transformation of lives in prison by The Holy Spirit.

We traveled to Greensville Correctional Center (GRCC) in Virginia for the KAIROS prison ministry. Greensville Correctional Center is a large, state prison (roughly 4,000 men), and we were in S-3 which houses about 900 men. At one time, over half of the inmates were Muslims.

KAIROS Weekends are held Thursday evening to Sunday twice a year, for forty-two men. Even though we, the KAIROS team, just do our part, Jesus runs the program. It's amazing to watch the Holy Spirit recapture souls, as many convert to Christianity or accept Jesus as their Savior and Lord.

While I was in Virginia serving on the KAIROS S-3 prison ministry team, I was amazed that 100% of the men who attended, 100% of the time took the Christian cross on a chain around their neck on Sunday morning, even though over half were Muslims, as well as Wiccans, atheists, Christians, etc. I have never witnessed so many mass conversions in my life. Prisons are a fertile ground to assist the Holy Spirit in recapturing souls.

The leader of the KAIROS Weekend prayed about who should give which talk, and the Holy Spirit chose me to give the first talk. I was very surprised, since I was a new team member, and this was a key talk. I have made many mistakes in my life, and most of the guys could identify with the mistakes that I have made. There is an uplifting message towards the end of the talk, and guidance on how to avoid these mistakes. Many were moved by my talk, which demonstrated The Holy Spirit starting to work internally on them. It's not me.

I could also feel the presence of evil spirits in the prison. I started to ask myself whether I should continue to go in the prisons anymore. After returning home, I asked my prayer partner at work to pray with me to ensure that no evil spirits were in me. We prayed in earnest, so that there wasn't even a minor spot of evil within me.

Then I saw Jesus, in a vision, put his arm around my shoulder and kiss my forehead. Because *Jesus kissed my forehead* and the many conversions to Christianity, I knew that I wanted to continue to be a part of the KAIROS prison ministry.

I have read in The Holy Bible where Jesus would pray through the night; see Luke 6:12 below.

Now it came to pass in those days that He went out to the mountain to pray, and continued all night in prayer to God.

I have tried to pray through the night, but I fell asleep. I wondered if anyone has actually prayed through the night. I finally met someone who prayed constantly, and he was in Greensville prison. This man of God at first prayed for fifty others every day. He continued to increase the number that he prayed for, and the last time I saw him, he was up to 3,200 names every day and night! He doesn't get much sleep, but he has done this for a long time. His prayers impacted others, both inside and outside the prison, even though he is behind the walls of a prison. I feel blessed to know him and pray for his family.

The men in prison come from all walks of life, some are intelligent, some have college degrees, and some have high level skills. Some have confessed their mistakes and crimes to Jesus, Jesus forgave them, and they accepted Jesus as their Lord and Savior. Some of the men will never be released out of prison, so their ministry is within the walls of the prison.

My experience with the KAIROS prison ministry was that it had a positive impact on the state prisons, such as Greensville Correctional Center. State prisons in in Virginia with a KAIROS prison ministry usually have fewer problems, less turnover of Correctional Officers, and much lower recidivism. I learned that those who attended the KAIROS Weekend, at least when I was a member of the KAIROS team, experienced a recidivism rate below 20% versus over 80% for those who don't attend the KAIROS Weekend.

There are many wonderful stories of those who attended the KAIROS Weekend. Forgiveness is a cornerstone of Christianity, as well as in the KAIROS program. Many men in prison, who don't attend KAIROS, think about settling scores when they are released, commit a crime, and then return to prison. Those who attend KAIROS usually forgive those who have wrong them, and also ask Jesus to forgive themselves. What a wonderful program.

On a KAIROS Weekend, the man sitting to my right was fifty-eight years old, who had been in prison for twenty-nine years and would be released in a few years. He couldn't understand why I would take vacation days from work to be with him and others in prison that I don't know. I told him that it's because of Jesus. He had been thinking of settling the score with two guys when he walks out of prison. But during the KAIROS Weekend, he forgave those two guys plus himself! *That saved his life as well as the lives of those two other guys. Jesus can do anything!*

While enjoying KAIROS, I started to experience Jesus in a different way at church.

Visions of Jesus at Church and Canoe-Like Ride

Nancy and I joined a wonderful church in northern Virginia that has a great preacher and an outstanding choir. As the choir sang, I closed my eyes seeking Jesus. As I was in this heavenly state of mind, I was able to see the clouds part, and Jesus would be there in the meadow, as I had seen Him before. This also reminded me of Steven in Acts 7:55-56:

> But he, being full of the Holy Spirit, gazed into heaven and saw the glory of God, and Jesus standing at the right hand of God, and said, "Look! I see the heavens opened and the Son of Man standing at the right hand of God!"

No one at the church ever asked me why my eyes were closed during church service. If they had, it would be another opportunity to tell them about my testimony of Jesus.

As I laid down to sleep at night, I have had several visions of traveling in a canoe-like boat into a cloud. This reminded me of a sign in the Ford Theater that said Abraham Lincoln had a dream of riding in a boat towards a shore. My vision was somewhat similar.

The first time when I had this dream of riding a canoe-like boat, I started to think about Nancy and my children. So, the dream ended, and I awoke and found that I was still on earth. Then, in the last vision, I wanted to go to Heaven without looking

back. I continued traveling in this canoe-like boat in this vision, but the boat-ride eventually faded away.

I can't wait to go to Heaven, but Jesus will decide when that will occur. In the meanwhile, I'll do my best to follow Jesus, do His will for my life, and tell my testimony.

Do you know if you will be going to Heaven when you die? If not, you can say out loud the prayer shown in the back of this book called "Altar Call" or attend a church that does altar calls.

After five plus years living in the Washington DC area, we had the opportunity to move back to the Midwest.

Weathering Storms

Our son-in-law experienced a stroke in his thirties, which left him unable to work. The federal agency in Washington DC allowed me to transfer my work location to Des Moines to help his family. I hired three experienced movers, who were homeless and lived in tents, to pack our stuff and load it into a large, U-Haul truck. With the help of a church friend, we drove our two vehicles and the U-Haul truck from northern Virginia to Des Moines over the next three days.

At the end of the first day, we heard tornado warnings on television of twenty plus tornados headed east that would meet us when we drove into Ohio the next day. So, we prayed to Jesus to calm the winds, and strangely, the next morning, the weather announcer said that the tornado winds had dissipated during the night and were no longer a factor! Thank-you Jesus!!

Several months later, Nancy had signed up for a vacation Bible school trip to Haiti for orphan girls. I noticed only two days before the group left, that a hurricane was headed directly for Haiti! As we met with the rest of the team and other church members that morning, we prayed as a group, for Jesus to calm the hurricane winds coming to Haiti, for good weather that week, and safe travels. Amazingly, the hurricane made a hard right, 90 degree turn and missed Haiti! Thank-you again Jesus.

The next summer, Nancy joined the same mission group to Haiti, and when they left to return home, she called me to ask me to pray for them. Their flight was delayed from landing in Miami, and they had only one hour to go through customs and make their connecting flight to Dallas. They would probably miss their connecting flight. So, I prayed, and when they reached the gate of their connecting flight to Dallas, it was announced that their pilots were delayed for two hours, so that they had ample time to make their flight. Thank-you Jesus!

We live on the ninth floor in a condo with floor to ceiling glass windows, which provide a good view of the downtown skyline. Recently, Nancy could not sleep well, so she got up around 4:00 am and went to the kitchen for a glass of water. As she looked out our glass windows towards the east, even though it was an overcast sky, she was amazed that there was one very bright star in the east. Then, she woke me up and told me that there was a very bright star in the sky, so I went to the window and noticed that there weren't any stars, moon, etc. because of the overcast sky; it was just dark blue. But, then I noticed there was just one star in the dark, blue sky, and it was the brightest star that I have ever witnessed in the sky.

We watched it for a while, and it did not move; therefore, it wasn't a jet, helicopter, or shooting star. This bright star reminded me of the Star of Bethlehem. See Matthew 2:9-11 below.

> When they heard the king, they departed; and behold, the star which they had seen in the East went before them, till it came and stood over where the young Child was. When they saw the star, they rejoiced with exceedingly great joy. And when they had come into the house, they saw the young Child with Mary His mother, and fell down and worshiped Him. And when they had opened their treasures, they presented gifts to Him: gold, frankincense, and myrrh.

The next night, I woke up at 4:24 am, and there was that same bright star in the east sky without any other stars or moon. I'm not sure what the bright star in the sky means, so I asked The Holy Spirit to reveal what this means. I did not receive a response. Could it be connected to Jesus coming back? I don't know, but I do know that when Jesus comes back, the sky will be dark, and He will shine brightly in the dark sky on a cloud. See Matthew 24:29 - 31 below.

> Immediately after the tribulation of those days the sun will be darkened, and the moon will not give its light; the stars will fall from heaven, and the powers of the heavens will be shaken. Then the sign of the Son of Man will appear in heaven, and then all the tribes of the earth will mourn, and they will see the Son of Man coming on the clouds of heaven with power and great glory. And He will send His angels with a great sound of a trumpet, and they will gather together His elect from the four winds, from one end of heaven to the other.

During our first winter in Des Moines, we traveled to Omaha to enjoy Christmas.

Feeling My Soul Dying

Nancy and I drove to Omaha to enjoy Christmas and attend "A Christmas Carol" with our son's family, which was wonderful. Afterwards, as we rode together on our way home, our grandson was watching a DVD movie about a man calling on evil forces to help fight and control others. As the movie started, I had a feeling that my soul was withdrawing and dying, and I felt like I was being suffocated. For survival, I asked if the sound and/or movie could be turned off. He started to use earplugs, and turned off the sound. It was now quiet, and I turned my head so that my eyes would not see it, and then my soul started to be revived.

Be careful of what you are watching and listening to whether it is a movie, internet, computers, cell phones, etc., since it does impact you spiritually! I have noticed that Jesus and the Holy Spirit come to me in visions, thoughts, etc. during the evenings when our place is quiet – no TV, no computers, no cell phones, and no internet. This also reminds me that Satan is the prince of the air. See Ephesians 2:1-3 below. I added the underlining.

> And you *He made alive,* who were dead in trespasses and sins, in which you once walked according to the course of this world, according to the <u>prince of the power of the air,</u> the spirit who now works in the sons of disobedience, among whom also we all once conducted ourselves in the lusts of our flesh, fulfilling the desires of the flesh

and of the mind, and were by nature children of wrath, just as the others.

In addition to movies, TV programs, internet, etc. Satan and his demons seem to also use alcohol, drugs, sex, anger, lies, and pride, to influence and control people.

But The Holy Spirit is more powerful than Satan and any demon.

Do you or your children watch or listen to ungodly movies, music, internet websites, or sexting? That will affect you and your children's relationship with Jesus in a very negative way. Is your family dysfunctional? Read The Holy Bible out loud as a family and see the difference it makes.

After the Christmas season, I sought out opportunities to serve the homeless in Des Moines.

Bible Study at a Homeless Shelter

The Holy Spirit used me as a vessel to start a Bible Study at a sizable homeless shelter in Des Moines. I asked a friend at church to help me in running the Bible Study. On the first night, no one attended, and the projector froze up midway into the DVD "The Star of Bethlehem". I went home, determined more than ever, to find out what was causing the problem with the DVD and lack of people attending, so I prayed to The Holy Spirit.

That night, The Holy Spirit revealed to me that He (The Holy Spirit) would lead the Bible Study and lead the fight against the evil spirits. Then, I felt this tingling sensation throughout my body three distinct times. Yes, I understood that The Holy Spirit would lead the fight against the evil spirits and lead the Bible Study. Fantastic! Then, the DVD's worked and homeless people started to attend the Bible Studies. Thank you Holy Spirit.

Then, I felt drawn to conduct an altar call. See attachment at the end of this book called "Altar Calls. So, I taught about Heaven and hell from The Holy Bible, and asked if anyone wanted to accept Jesus as their Lord and Savior. Four of the eleven attendees stood up, repeated the words of the altar call, and accepted Jesus as their Lord and Savior!

I also taught forgiveness based on scriptures. See the forgiveness talk at the end of the book. At the end of the forgiveness talk, tears flowed and Kleenex was used to wipe them away as The Holy Spirit worked within their hearts, and they forgave others and asked Jesus to forgive themselves. See Matthew 6:14-15:

> "For if you forgive men their trespasses, your heavenly Father will also forgive you. But if you do not forgive men their trespasses, neither will your Father forgive your trespasses.

Anger has caused much unforgiveness that people, including myself, have carried around. Sometimes, it has taken several times of forgiving others, before that memory is gone. For one homeless woman, she was troubled by the man who caused her to be homeless. I told her that she could start forgiving him by writing his name on the rice paper and dropping it into the bowl of forgiveness, which she did. The rice paper will dissolve in the water, symbolizing that your sin of unforgiveness is gone. A few weeks later, she found someone willing to open their door and take her in, and she left the shelter.

Praying for those that you have forgiven, telling them that you forgive them, or asking others to forgive you can be a tough step to take, but it helps. Not forgiving others, who have wronged you, does nothing to them. They carry on as if nothing happened, and it will just tear you up on the inside. But when you forgive them, then all of that weight is off your shoulders, and you feel like a new person. Try it, and see if that doesn't happen to you. Besides, our Father in Heaven won't forgive us until we forgive others. Read Romans 12:19.

> Do not take revenge, my dear friends, but leave room for God's wrath, for it is written: It is mine to avenge, I will repay, says the Lord.

I leave vengeance to Jesus. I need not to judge others, even when they mistreat me. This, at times, is difficult for me to do, but I know that Jesus will judge them, and I don't want to be judged. That's for sure!

I was teaching about the seven seals in chapter 6 of Revelations. Most were so engrossed in the scriptures that they didn't eat the cookies. After class was over, one woman broke out singing praises to Jesus, then everyone else left the room, except for one man who approached me. He told me that he was very fearful of someone following him. He imagined that he wanted to kill him. I told him that fear comes from evil spirits, not God.

The Holy Spirit was encouraging me to help him. I asked him if he wanted to expel his fear, and he said yes. So, I placed my hand on him, and said by the authority of Jesus Christ, The Holy Bible, and the power of The Holy Spirit, I commanded the fear to leave him. When I said this a third time, I felt a surge of power, like lightening, go down my arm into him. I also told him to get on his knees tonight, confess his sins, and ask Jesus for forgiveness. He was noticeably much better the next Tuesday night.

Then, another guy wanted a ride home, and told me that he researched pagan gods and then evil, sexual spirits attacked him at night. I asked him if he wanted these evil spirits of sex to be out of his life, and he said yes. So, I asked The Holy Spirit to cast these evil spirits out of him, and to get on his knees tonight, confess your sins, and ask Jesus for forgiveness. What an evening! This was the first time that I have been involved in casting out evil spirits.

We live on the ninth floor of a building in a relatively small condo with a balcony that overlooks downtown Des Moines. A young eagle landed on our balcony railing and just remained there. Small birds flew close to the young eagle and were trying to pick at and bother the eagle. The young eagle would just raise one foot/claw and look at the closest bird on the railing. We were excited about seeing the young eagle just a few feet away from us. The young eagle calmly stayed there on our balcony railing as we took a few pictures. The thought came to me that this young eagle may somehow reflect my growth and maturity in Jesus.

Young Eagle on Our Balcony Rail

In addition to the Bible Study at the homeless shelter, I discovered a group of people serving homeless people on Sunday afternoons. They serve the homeless in tents, abandon houses, cars, garages, and apartments delivering food, personal hygiene items, some clothes, and occasionally tents. The homeless were usually glad to see us, since they appreciated our friendliness and food.

At first, I volunteered almost every Sunday afternoon on all of the different routes, just to know the homeless people, their personalities, and to learn where all of the homeless live. I would ask if they needed prayers, and usually most of them wanted prayers for healing, jobs, broken relationships, etc. There are some who don't want to pray, but most of them are Christians. Since they need hope and a real change in their lives, they usually ask for prayers and will also offer up their own prayers.

Some are not welcomed in churches, but most don't attend church, since they don't have transportation. If churches offered transportation, food, minimal amounts of cash, as well as the good news of Jesus, they will come to church.

During the winter, we delivered propane tanks and heaters to those in tents, abandoned houses, garages etc. It's fun and the homeless really depend on this help. People living in tents can freeze to death if they don't have any heat during the bitterly cold, winter weather. In early January, there were days forecasted with below zero, so we delivered propane tanks twice that week. A group of volunteers prayed to Jesus asking Him to bring warmer weather for the homeless living in tents, cars, etc. Unseasonably, warm weather arrived for the next several weeks. Thank-you Jesus again!

Jesus can and does alter the weather if you pray. This reminds of what Jesus said in Matthew 21:22.

> And whatever things you ask in prayer, believing, you will receive.

I met two volunteers that are also involved in prison ministry in Iowa, and I joined this group of men who go into Iowa state prisons. Men in prison are searching for answers, and Jesus is the perfect answer.

Iowa Prison Ministry

Prison ministry is so worthwhile, just by letting Jesus' light shine through us and telling them about Jesus. I have served as a team member in three Iowa state prisons. We had over ninety attendees at one weekend event.

One man asked me about the voice of Jesus. See John 10:27 below.

> My sheep hear My voice, and I know them, and they follow Me.

I told him that it's a voice that comes from within. It's not a voice that you hear with your ears. It's distinctly different. I can't really describe it very well, but you will have no problems hearing Him. Then, I compare it with what I have read in The Holy Bible, and it's always in sync. I know His voice well enough to know that it's Jesus.

There have been physical healings occur during our weekend events in prisons. One man had a badly mangled leg that gave him constant pain. He could barely walk with a cane, and usually just stayed seated, until he left to go back to his cell. We laid hands on him, and commanded the pain to leave. He arrived the next morning, without any pain, and was walking around with a smile and no cane. Everyone was amazed.

Another man at our table had relationship problems with his family. For some of those in prison, their family members are a large part of the problem. He had not seen his sister for roughly twenty years. On Saturday afternoon, he said that he needed to see his sister, who lives about 60 miles away, to mend the broken relationship. She arrived shortly after he said he needed to see her! He didn't know that she was coming. They talked through the issues, and now she will help him. He was amazed and smiling.

A number of the guys are baptized for the first time during the four-day event, and others rededicated their baptism. I often wondered what their lives would have been like, if they would have accepted Jesus in their heart and been baptized in high school.

I'm a bottom-line type of guy, and I want to summarize what I have learned so far about God.

Write Down Your Thoughts, Notes, and Comments Here

Part Four: Bottom Line Lessons

And this is eternal life, that they may know You, the only true God, and Jesus Christ whom You have sent.

John 17:3

God is Real

Remember a few years ago, when people went to a movie and many died. I read where one young man said that he was devastated, because the movies provide "hope".

My hope and your hope are not in the movies, a job, the President, Social Security, 401K, etc. *Our hope is in Jesus. He is REAL!!! God is so good, so powerful, so all knowing.*

I'm not just saying it – I know it!

When I pray to The Holy Spirit for help, The Holy Spirit normally reveals wisdom and knowledge while I am asleep or almost asleep. Sometimes, The Holy Spirit instructs me through the entire night. The Holy Spirit is awe inspiring. I love Him. He is so kind, nice, and detailed in His guidance.

Some Christians, who have accepted Jesus Christ as their Lord and Savior, but do not pray to The Holy Spirit, they don't talk to The Holy Spirit, they don't ask for help, they don't ask The Holy Spirit to explain scripture. In short, they don't know The Holy Spirit! The Holy Spirit brings incredible joy in my heart! He also will bring to my mind sin in my life and names of people that I need to forgive. I feel sad for these Christians who have not felt this incredible joy, truth, and wisdom from The Holy Spirit.

The Holy Spirit is an incredible helper, teacher, guidance counselor, and so much more. See John 14:26.

> But the Helper, the Holy Spirit, whom the Father will send in My name, He will teach you all things, and bring to your remembrance all things that I said to you.

The Holy Spirit will guide you. See John 16:13.

> However, when He, the Spirit of truth, has come, He will guide you into all truth; for He will not speak on His own *authority,* but whatever He hears He will speak; and He will tell you things to come.

I encourage everyone to call upon The Holy Spirit daily to help you, to teach you, and your life will never be the same. You will not worry about anything; you will not be afraid of anything; it's a totally different life. You will smile again, and be able to help others by using the power of The Holy Spirit.

While in Washington D.C., Nancy was traveling on the metro to go shopping. She stopped at Macy's and misplaced her keys. She called me in distress, and so we prayed together on the phone. In about fifteen minutes, even though there were hundreds of people in the store, a woman came up to Nancy and asked her if she was missing some keys. She quickly responded yes, and the woman gave her the keys! The Holy Spirit is unbelievable!

Earlier I stated that I was baptized in The Holy Spirit. As they laid their hands on my back, our table leader Tim asked The Holy Spirit to come into my body, and that's exactly what happened. Then, I was in the Spirit for the first time in my life. I could see inside my body as my heart literally did a summersault! Then, bolts of lightning surged throughout my body causing a buzzing noise. At that moment, I didn't know if I was dead or alive. So, I paused and placed my hands on my knees and could feel my hands pinching my knees. Then I knew that I was alive! I knew that I wasn't asleep or in a dream; I was awake; it was real. I was completely wrapped up in The Holy Spirit. I could see from the outside that I was in a large, dark brown cocoon. Inside, it felt soft like cotton. Those are the closest words that I can use to describe what happened.

Let's analyze what happened when I was baptized in The Holy Spirit.

- The day before I was baptized in The Holy Spirit, I cried out loud asking Jesus to forgive me for very specific sins I had committed!
- The night that I was baptized in The Holy Spirit, I was praying on my knees. The Holy Spirit taught me this! It's very important to be humble.
- Our table leader asked the Holy Spirit to come into my body, to fill me up, my heart, mind, body, and soul. Have you asked the Holy Spirit to come into your body, heart, mind, and soul? A well-known minister on TV asked The Holy Spirit to come into his body, and that's what happened.
- Multiple guys were praying. Form small prayer groups and try it.
- Prayers were verbalized out loud. Be brutally honest out loud with God with your words and emotions. The Holy Spirit has told me to pray with all of my heart. Ask Jesus to do His will through you; to use you as His vessel. Believe in your prayers – anticipate and expect an answer from God!
- Here's a tip. Write out your prayer. Then read it out loud to Jesus. This will be the start of your prayer journal. Then read your previous week's journal. See if your prayer was answered. After a few months, group your prayers into categories. See if certain events/thoughts trigger certain type of prayers.

- The Holy Spirit is your personal Teacher, Counselor, Friend, and Advisor. Use Him! Pray to the Holy Spirit! Talk to Him! Ask Him questions. Before making a decision, ask the Holy Spirit!!! I believe that God's job is to decide what we should do, and it's our job to do it. It's that simple.

The Holy Spirit is real. Take your faith seriously and work at it. There is nothing more important or as rewarding. Also, The Holy Spirit revealed to me that The Holy Bible is completely true. No one completely knows everything in The Holy Bible, and that is good. I trust and believe in The Holy Bible. If I have questions, I ask The Holy Spirit to teach me.

Jesus is REAL. He is alive and doing wonderful things in this world. You can know Jesus by first opening your heart to Jesus and asking Him to come into your heart. Say the "Altar Call" out loud as shown in the back of this book.

If you have Jesus in your heart, you'll love reading The Holy Bible. You can understand Jesus by reading The Holy Bible each day. You will learn about God by reading The Holy Bible, and you'll also learn who we are, and what we need to do. Read slowly a chapter a day starting in Matthew, Mark, etc. until you finish the New Testament. Then, read Genesis, etc. Join a Bible class. Reading the Holy Bible is life changing. Your life will be focused on serving Him, and you will think of Him.

You will want to follow Jesus' commandments, because you love Jesus. I have found some of the commandments difficult to follow, so I ask The Holy Spirit to help me. I ask The Holy Spirit to wipe all unclean thoughts out of my mind, cleanse my heart, and to totally wipe out of my memory bank all unclean thoughts. I don't want those unclean thoughts to come back ever again. Reading scripture and singing hymns also will cleanse your mind.

God is REAL! Get to know Him, and then tell others about Jesus.

Help the Homeless

I'm not sure that I could live in a tent without running water, a shower, heat, air conditioning, or a bathroom for any extended time and deal with flies, mosquitoes, raccoons, snakes, etc. Yet, there are generations of families living in tents, because they cannot afford apartments even with regular employment.

Then to find your clothes in the dark, walk to McDonalds or Wal-Mart to use the bathroom, brush your teeth, shave, etc., then walk to a bus stop with the right change, arrive at work with a cheerful smile, work, and then wait for a bus, and walk through the woods to your tent! Whew! Or if the weather is cold, raining, or extremely hot, walking to the closest mall, sitting in the mall, until you are forced to leave. Most stores will call the police if they view homeless people asking for money.

Over half of the homeless have jobs, but just arriving to work on time with clean clothes involves a lot of time and energy to clean-up, ride their bicycle, ride a bus, or walk to work. Have you thought that the man or woman who waits on you at a restaurant, bags your groceries, park your car, etc. may be homeless? Parked cars that look really messy inside with lots of papers, clothes, etc. probably have someone living there. Plus, it's difficult to apply for a job, if you don't have an address or cell phone.

For example, if a one-bedroom apartment costs $ 1,200 per month, food costing $350 per month, plus utilities, transportation, medicine, etc. and a person only makes $ 10 per hour, they would have to work over 100 hours per week to pay the bills. You can try different cost assumptions, but the point is that it is very difficult to earn enough money for an apartment, food, medicine, etc. if you are making minimum wage, unless the landlord allows several people to room together by sleeping on the floor.

I help as many homeless people as I can. For example, I sold my 4Runner to a wonderful man for $ 1.00, who was living in a tent. He needed transportation to get to his job and back to his tent, plus the vehicle allowed him to get married and live in an apartment. He now has a wonderful family, and leads the Bible Study at a homeless shelter.

People have asked me how they can help the homeless. I recommend that you and a friend go together, pray to Jesus for safety and guidance, meet someone who is homeless, ask them what their first name is, and what they like to do.

Tell your testimony about Jesus in your life, and encourage them to tell you their testimony. Testifying about God is so much fun, because God places so much joy in your heart, and it's remembering these experiences. They will let you know how you can help them. It might be a ride, money, food, clothes, etc. By knowing them, then you will feel more comfortable with them, and they will feel more comfortable with you.

If you want someone to live in your spare bedroom:

- Be sure that they are a Christian. See 2 John 10 below.
  If anyone comes to you and does not bring this doctrine, do not receive him into your house nor greet him;

- Do not allow anyone to drink alcohol (beer, liquor, wine) or take drugs, and tell them to ask first before using or taking something.

- Bluntly state your house rules before they move in.
- Ask them to follow your house rules.

If they break your rules, don't hesitate to show them the door, and although they won't like it, they will understand.

Do you feel a need to help the homeless? Be sure to tell them about Jesus in addition to helping them.

Who is in Control?

I trust that you have been inspired by my testimonies of how Jesus and The Holy Spirit have wonderfully impacted my life.

If you would like to be closer to Jesus, then I would ask you the following questions:

Have you accepted Jesus as your Lord and Savior, regardless if you have attended church? Have you confessed that you are a sinner and accepted Jesus as your Lord and Savior? If not, then do it today. Contact your minister or the closest Protestant Christian Church. Tell the minister that you want to accept Jesus as your Lord and Savior.

If you haven't been baptized or if you can't remember your baptism, then you need to be baptized. Go to your local Christian church and ask to be baptized.

Who makes the decisions in your life? If you make your own decisions, I would strongly encourage you to get on your knees, tell Jesus that you want to turn all control to Him and completely surrender to Jesus. Then, before you make a major decision, pray to Jesus and ask Him which way you should go. If you don't receive an answer, then read The Holy Bible for an answer to your decision. If you still cannot find an answer, then search your heart and move forward.

I have found that even if I don't receive an answer, the results are better if I pray first, than not asking Jesus.

Next Steps

I strongly encourage everyone to believe in and accept Jesus as their Lord (means that you live your life according to His commandments) and Savior (Jesus saves people from hell). If you will confess your sins, ask Jesus for forgiveness, and accept Jesus as your Lord and Savior in your heart, by the blood of Jesus you will be saved and go to Heaven. Salvation is the number one goal in your life, while you are still alive on this earth.

The next step is water baptism by a minister or a disciple of Jesus.

The third step is baptism in The Holy Spirit. Have a couple of disciples lay hands on you, in prayer ask that you may receive The Holy Spirit, then receive The Holy Spirit.

What I'm saying is written in Acts 8:14-17 as shown below:

> 14 Now when the apostles who were at Jerusalem heard that Samaria had received the word of God, they sent Peter and John to them, 15 who, when they had come down, prayed for them that they might receive the Holy Spirit. 16 For as yet He had fallen upon none of them. They had only been baptized in the name of the Lord Jesus. 17 Then they laid hands on them, and they received The Holy Spirit.

Here's how I view these scriptures:

- Verse 14 - they received the word of God. Faith comes from hearing the Word.
- Verse 16 – water baptism.
- Verses 15 and 17 – baptized into The Holy Spirit
  - Verse 15 - prayed to receive The Holy Spirit.
  - Verse 17 – Laid hands on them, and they received The Holy Spirit.

I encourage you to receive salvation, water baptism, and then be baptized in The Holy Spirit.

My story is fun to tell others, but it doesn't compare to reading The Holy Bible if you are a believer. Read The Holy Bible each and every day. Read it slowly each day, so that the words of God slowly soak into your mind and heart. Read the cross referenced scriptures for increased understanding; the words will jump out at you, and come alive.

Forgive others every day, and ask Jesus to forgive you. Ask The Holy Spirit for help, to teach you, and guide you. You will live a different life. You will smile more often, you will no longer worry nor fear anything, and you will be a new person.

> Therefore, if anyone is in Christ, he is a new creation; the old is gone, the new has come. 2 Corinthians 5:17.

Are you ready for a new, positive life? Try it and see for yourself.

Write Down Your Thoughts, Notes, and Comments Here

Part Five:
Attachments

But sanctify the Lord God in your hearts, and always *be* ready to *give* a defense to everyone who asks you a reason for the hope that is in you, with meekness and fear;

1 Peter 3:15

Attachments

I have included the following attachments, so that you may use them. First is the altar call, then a talk on forgiveness, seeking God, and the contact information for the two homeless shelters mentioned in the book. The Nehemiah House in Virginia is currently needing funds to start building.

Altar Call

Below is the altar call (prayer of salvation) that I have used. It's based on Romans 10:9-10.

> "That if you confess with your mouth, "Jesus is Lord," and believe in your heart that God raised Him from the dead, you will be saved. For with the heart one believes unto righteousness, and with the mouth confession is made unto salvation."

Prayer of Salvation – Say it & Mean it!

> ***"Jesus, I know that I have broken your laws and my sins have separated me from you. I am truly sorry, and now I want to turn away from my past sinful life toward you. Please forgive me, and help me avoid sinning again. I believe that you are the Son of God; you died for my sins, resurrected from the dead, alive, and hears my prayer. I invite you, Jesus, to become the Lord of my life, wash me with Your blood, to rule and reign in my heart from this day forward. Please send Your Holy Spirit to help me obey You, and to do Your will for the rest of my life. Please Holy Spirit come into my heart and my body. In Jesus' name I pray. Amen."***

Therefore, if anyone is in Christ, he is a new creation; the old is gone, the new has come. 2 Corinthians 5:17.

Forgiveness Talk

Note before starting the forgiveness talk.

The forgiveness talk can be a very powerful spiritual experience, based on my experience, since it's run by Jesus and The Holy Spirit. I have seen many hardened hearts melt by The Holy Spirit during this talk. Have Kleenex available, since tears are normally shed.

The following forgiveness talk uses pocket-size sheets of paper, as well as the cross or a bowl of water. If you use a large bowl of water (with red dye if you wish to represent that their sins of unforgiveness are covered by the blood of Jesus), rice paper works well and will disappear as a person stirs the water with a large ladle spoon. If you use a cross, then just regular pocket-size sheets of paper can be used, where the people place their lists of names at the base of the cross.

Be sure that the atmosphere of the room is in quiet reverence for God. It is a holy time for serious contemplation. This talk can be combined with communion. If you conduct communion, after people drop their list of names into the bowl or at the base of the cross, then the minister can give them communion.

I use a bold voice and a steady rate of speech with emotion. Prayers are indented and shown in bold font. Below is the start of the forgiveness talk.

Forgiveness Talk

Please bow your heads as we pray to the Holy Spirit.

Come, Holy Spirit, fill the hearts of your faithful and kindle in them the fire of your love. Send forth your spirit and they shall be created. And you shall renew the face of the earth. O God, who by the light of the Holy Spirit did instruct the hearts of the faithful, grant that by the same Holy Spirit we may be truly wise and ever enjoy your consolations. Through Christ our Lord. Amen.

In Matthew 6:9-13 is the Lord's Prayer, but notice the next two verses 14 and 15, Jesus emphasizes that:

For if you forgive other people when they sin against you, your heavenly Father will also forgive you. But if you do not forgive others their sins, your Father will not forgive your sins.

In Acts, Paul left Ephesus knowing that the Holy Spirit was guiding him to Jerusalem for an uncertain fate. Paul knows that Jesus died on the cross at Jerusalem. Paul knows that he may die on the cross. At Jerusalem, The Holy Spirit tells Paul that he must go to Rome. See Acts 19:21 below.

When these things were accomplished, Paul purposed in the Spirit, when he had passed through Macedonia and Achaia, to go to Jerusalem, saying, "After I have been there, I must also see Rome.

Paul, like Jesus, is on his way to the cross. Some of us have walked here this morning, some have driven here, and we too are on our journey to the cross. What happened at the cross? Jesus died for the forgiveness of our sins. That is great news!

As a follower of Jesus Christ, I believe forgiveness is critical for us to be obedient to God. I made mistakes. You made mistakes. For us to move closer to God, we must first forgive others, ask others to forgive us, and then ask Jesus to forgive us.

The Holy Bible is filled with statements assuring us that God forgave us of anything which we might have done or said, if we are willing to ask for that forgiveness and to accept it.

Listen to the word of God:

- As far as the east is from the west, so far does He remove our sins from us. Psalm 103:12.
- This is My blood which seals God's covenant, My blood poured out for many for the forgiveness of sins. Matthew 26:28.
- But if we confess our sins to God, He will keep His promise and do what is right: He will forgive our sins and purify us from all wrong doing. 1 John 1:9.

I don't know about you, but for me, that is good news!

As a kid, I noticed that the guys who just loved to fight were mostly Italian. I also know that if you want to preach the good news of Jesus Christ and want to fight about it, go to Israel. Others have done that and were accosted. Or go to many Muslim countries, and you may end up in jail or dead. Therefore, when we read about Paul going to jail, beaten, etc., it's understandable.

What you say out loud with your lips is in your heart. What is said here; stays here. It's a safe room.

(Insert your personal story of you not forgiving other people.)

As we learned in the story of the Prodigal Son, God values us this much no matter what we have done. Some of us find that hard to believe, but The Holy Bible insists that God loved us so much that He gave His Only Son to die for us, and that He did that even while we were still sinners.

When we refuse to seek and accept God's forgiveness, we are really admitting that we don't want to be new creatures, because if we accept it, He will make new creatures out of us.

In the final analysis, it is probably our enormous pride which keeps us from accepting forgiveness. In our self-centeredness, we see our evil, sinful acts, as being so exceptional, so great, that what God did for us is not enough to wipe away such sin.

We are, in fact, saying "Jesus, you haven't done enough for me yet. Get back on the cross, because You dying that way was not enough to answer for what I have done." Wow! Think about that.

Jesus goes to emphasize this point by saying, "If you forgive others the wrongs they have done to you, God will also forgive you. But if you do not forgive others, then God will not forgive the wrongs you have done."

What is forgiveness?

First of all, forgiveness is something you do. It is not just a change in feelings about another person. Forgiving others means giving their imperfect humanity to God and admitting that beginning the long forgiveness process cannot be done without God's help.

We humans like to hold on to our anger, but with God, we can begin letting go of our anger and start to free ourselves from these bonds. It now becomes your decision to stop treating another person as though they owed you something. It is your promise made to God to stop blaming someone for something. Failure to forgive can destroy our lives. It takes all of our energy we might have for something good and eats away at us. Forgiveness is a choice, a decision which may have to be made over and over again until the process is completed.

But in the end, for our own sake and in obedience to the Lord we love, we make that decision to forgive. It doesn't necessarily mean that our feelings change. We may make that decision to forgive even when we are boiling with anger. God knows.

> **Please bow your head as we pray: "God, you know how angry I am at this person. You know that if I could get my hands on him/her I would choke him/her. But I forgive him/her, because You have asked me to do so. I forgive him/her out of obedience to You, Father, and I hold him/her up to You and pray for good for him/her. I pray also that You fill me with Your love and compassion and understanding for him/her. Amen."**

This is a prayer that He never fails to answer.

God can change our hearts about the people we hold in unforgiveness. I know that, because He's changed mine. It is hard to believe when our anger and hatred are so great that anything can help. But, God can help. He can make a new creature out of us.

Sometimes, the people who hurt us most are the ones closest to us, the ones we love the most, the ones we trust the most. Jesus had that problem with Judas, and even with Peter. He's still having it with me, maybe even with some of you. We have to keep forgiving, just as God has to keep forgiving us.

I am going to ask you to do something. (pause) If you have anyone you hold in unforgiveness – your father, mother, your brother, your sister, all those people who have failed to see Jesus in you, to see you as a person of supreme importance to God...the officer who arrested you, the person or persons who witnessed against you, the guy/woman who gives you a rough time, all of those who feel they are superior to you, anyone you hate because of prejudice or pride, the person who doesn't forgive you.

If you hold any of these people in unforgiveness, I am asking you to write their names down on the sheet of paper I am passing out to you. I also ask you to ask the Holy Spirit to bring to your mind the names of anyone whom you might have overlooked. Keep the sheet in front of you and as names come to you, add them to the list. No one else will see this list except you and God, so don't be afraid to write down the names which come to you. Let's just pause a minute and ask our Lord to bring these names to our minds. Please pray with me:

> **Dear God, please bring to my mind the name of any person for whom I harbor ill will, whom I hold unforgiven, and Father help me to understand that it makes no difference if I am still angry with that person, for I can't change the way I feel about him or about her, but You can.**
>
> **Continue to feed me these names, Lord, I ask in Jesus name. Amen.**

Go ahead and write names on the sheet of paper.

> (Pause for a few minutes to allow them to write their names down)

Then ask everyone to bow their heads in prayer.

> **Merciful and Almighty God, here are my names... the names which I believe You have brought to my mind.**

> **Lord, You know how I feel about these people, and some of those feelings are certainly not expressive of Your love.**
>
> **I forgive them and pray for good for them, Father, and I ask You to forgive me for my unforgiveness of them.**
>
> **Fill me with Your love and compassion for them. Remove any anger or resentment which I might have in my heart and heal our relationship.**
>
> **I ask this, Father, in Jesus' name. Amen.**

Please bow your head for silent contemplation of your lists. (walk away)

When you are prepared to forgive those people on your list, come up, offer your list to the Lord, and place it (at the base of the cross or in the bowl of water, depending on which one you use).

(After everyone has brought forward their list of names, and if communion is not conducted, then close with the following prayer.)

Please pray with me the following prayer:

> **Lord Jesus Christ, You have taught me to pray: Forgive us our trespasses as we forgive those who trespass against us.**
>
> **In Your name, I am to repair the broken relationship. I am to mend the broken. I am to welcome back the wanderer who returns.**

Lord Jesus Christ, help me to understand that this power is Your power to be used for the sake of those for whom You died.

Help me to understand that I cannot turn away from any who ask for forgiveness or need my forgiveness. Help me to understand my denial of unforgiveness!

Help me to overcome any hindrance that would keep me from sharing the fullness and the power of Your saving and forgiving grace.

I ask it in the power of your name. Amen.

Seeking God

Note before starting this talk about seeking God.

Praying and receiving responses from God will be a life changer. I sincerely and fervently pray that others will experience Jesus and The Holy Spirit.

SEEKING GOD

- QUIET MEDITATION – CENTER ON GOD

Get on Our Knees and bow our heads in prayer – Lord, open our hearts and minds by the power of your Holy Spirit, that, as the Scriptures are read and Your Word proclaimed, we may hear with joy what you say to us today. Amen.

(Sing one of your favorite church hymns. One of my favorite hymns is "Holy, Holy, Holy! Lord God Almighty".)

At some time in the future, you and I may no longer be here. So, I want to tell what I have learned from my spiritual journey.

Do you remember a few years ago, when people went to a movie, and many died. I read where one young man said that he was devastated, because the movies provide "hope".

My hope and your hope are not in the movies, a job, the President, etc. It's in Jesus, our Father, and the Holy Spirit. Jesus, our Father, and the Holy Spirit is REAL!!! God is so good, so powerful, so all knowing.

I'm not just saying it – I know it!

When I tell my experiences with God, people are amazed! They are encouraged! I truly want everyone to have a close relationship with Jesus, the Holy Spirit, and our Father. I also want you to know that The Holy Bible is true!

Before I tell you about some of my experiences with God, what experiences have you had with God? Go ahead and share the moments that you have had with God.

(Wait and listen)

Do you wonder why God answers some people's prayers and not others? Why is it that some people have awesome experiences and others just wait? Some people know what God's purpose is for their life, and others aren't really sure.

Let's see what The Holy Bible says. Please open your Holy Bible to:

- **James 4:8**

    Draw near to God and He will draw near to you. Cleanse *your* hands, *you* sinners; and purify *your* hearts, *you* double-minded.

- **Matthew 5:8**

    Blessed *are* the pure in heart,
    For they shall see God.

I added the underline in the above scripture. How can we be pure in heart and soul? The next scripture reference provides further insight.

- **Psalm 66:18**

  If I regard iniquity in my heart·
  The Lord will not hear.

God doesn't hear your prayer if you have sin in your heart. Repent, confess, and ask for forgiveness to clean up your heart.

- **Deuteronomy 4:29-31**

  But from there you will seek the Lord your God, and you will <u>find *Him*</u> if you seek Him with all your heart and with all your soul. (Underlining added.)

- **Deuteronomy 6:5**

  You shall love the Lord your God with all your heart, with all your soul, and with all your strength.

Know that The Holy Bible is completely true. Based on the scriptures above, we should have a clean heart, pray with all your heart and all your soul in seeking God. I have found that fasting, while in prayer, will often produce a closer relationship with Jesus. Do not have any doubt in your mind or heart; expect a response.

<u>(Insert your story about when you experienced God.)</u>
Based on my experience with God, I have noticed the following:

- Ask for forgiveness with all of your heart. Just prior to baptism in The Holy Spirit, I had cried out loud asking Jesus to forgive me for very specific sins I had committed!
- Then, I was on my knees. The Holy Spirit taught me this! It's very important to be humble.

- Have you asked the Holy Spirit to come into your body, heart, mind, soul? A well-known minister on television recently said that he had asked The Holy Spirit to come into his body, and apparently has had a wonderful experience with The Holy Spirit.
- My experience involved multiple Christians in prayer. Form small groups and try praying out loud in small groups.
- Verbally pray out loud and pray with your whole heart. Be brutally honest with God with your words and emotions.
- Here's a tip. Write out your prayer. Then read it out loud to Jesus. This will be the start of your prayer journal. Then read your previous week's journal. See if your prayer was answered. After a few months, group your prayers into categories. See if certain events/thoughts trigger certain type of prayers.
- The Holy Spirit is your personal Teacher, Counselor, Friend, Comforter, and Advisor. Use Him! Pray to the Holy Spirit! Talk to Him! Ask Him questions. Before making a decision, ask the Holy Spirit!!!

Now, I long for the Lord! My body, mind, and soul ache for Him, similar to what David said below.

Psalm 63:1
O God, You *are* my God;
Early will I seek You;
My soul thirsts for You;
My flesh longs for You
In a dry and thirsty land
Where there is no water.

I learned that The Holy Bible is not just a book – it's alive! After baptism in the Holy Spirit, I was on fire for Jesus. I thoroughly enjoyed, it was so much fun, reading The Holy Bible. I would read it slowly, stopping and thinking about the verse. Then, I wondered what it would be like to actually see that verse! The Holy Spirit transported me and gave me a front row seat, where I saw several guys in middle-eastern clothes standing next to some large rocks and talking. That was so cool! But it didn't seem as exciting as reading The Holy Bible. Then, the vision stopped, and I returned to reading The Holy Bible. The Holy Bible is alive!

Here's something that I have noticed. The majority of my visions come when I lay my head down at night to go to sleep. My eyes may be closed, but I am still awake. The TV is off, no music, no cell phone, and no computer. It's quiet. It's just me, the Holy Spirit, and Jesus. Then, I say repeatedly Jesus over and over again. I am mentally chasing Jesus by saying His name numerous times. Also, if I have asked The Holy Spirit for help in deciding what to do or what to say, usually The Holy Spirit provides answers in thoughts to my mind. Sometimes, The Holy Spirit will provide extremely detailed guidance throughout the night. Usually, I'm energized the next morning, even though The Holy Spirit may have been active with me throughout the night.

We're all creatures of habits. What do you do in the morning or before going to bed? On a sheet of paper, write down:

- What do you do on a regular basis in the morning? (Pause) What is your morning routine? Write down your answer. (Pause)
- What do you do during the last hour in the evening before you go to bed? Write down your answer. (Pause)

- If you want to love Jesus with all your heart and all of your soul, what should be your routine in the morning? Write down your answer. (Pause)
- If you want to search for Jesus with all your heart, what should you do in the last hour in the evening before going to bed? Write down you're answer. (Pause)

These are just my thoughts. I fervently want you to seek God with all your heart, with all your soul, and with your entire mind. See Matthew 22:37.

> Jesus said to him, "'You shall love the LORD your God with all your heart, with all your soul, and with all your mind.'

Try the suggestions above. You can do it, and come closer to Jesus. Your life will be forever changed, and so will the lives of your children.

To Contact The Refuge -
A Fresh Start in Minnesota or
The Nehemiah House in Virginia

The two homeless shelters that I mention in this book are the following two shelters.

If you want to make a donation to The Refuge – A Fresh Start in Marshall, MN, go to

> http://therefugemarshall.org/

Or send your donation in the mail to:

> WCA - The Refuge "A Fresh Start"
> 1400 S Saratoga
> Marshall MN 56258
> (507)537-1416

The Nehemiah House in Woodbridge, VA has been planned and is now raising funds to build the facility. If you want to make a donation, go to:

> http://www.nehemiahhouseva.org/

Or send your donation in the mail to:

Nehemiah House Project
c/o Robert Zanders
5755 Rhode Island Avenue
Woodbridge, VA 22193

Write Down Your Thoughts, Notes, and Comments Here

Daniel Evans

Jesus told Daniel to write his spiritual experiences in a book Jesus Is The Light In This Dark World. This book will:

- Inspire you.
- Captivate you, while you slowly absorb and ponder each chapter.

It's all true. Plus, all net proceeds will be donated to Christian homeless shelters.

Daniel is a servant for Jesus, who knows his purpose on earth is to help homeless people and write this book.

Daniel loves to tell his testimonies of Jesus and The Holy Spirit to congregations, mission committees, various organizations, or one-on-one encounters with strangers and friends. To contact Daniel:

www.Jesus-Is-The-Light.com
JesusIsTheLightInThisDarkWorld@gmail.com.

Please let me know if you have been impacted by this book, or if your Bible class is using this book. If you want to use this book as a fundraiser, let me know, and we'll work with you.

Jesus used Daniel to help start The Refuge – A Fresh Start in Marshall, Minnesota, as well as The Nehemiah House in Woodbridge, Virginia, CFIRE homeless outreach in

Washington D.C., a Bible Study at The Bill Mehr Drop-In Center in Woodbridge, Virginia, and a Bible Study at a homeless shelter in Des Moines, Iowa.

Daniel loves working as a team member for Walk to Emmaus and prison ministries.

Daniel has a wonderful wife Nancy, four grown children, and twelve grandchildren.

Printed in the United States
By Bookmasters